WORKBOOK

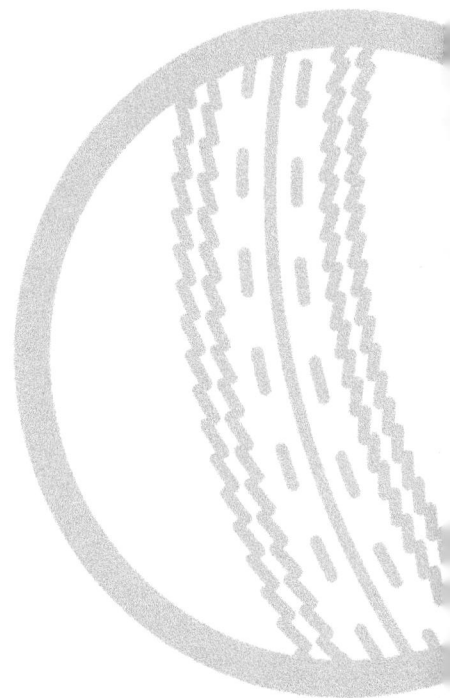

Play brave.
Play clever.
Play better.

Mindful Cricket.

From psychologist and best-selling author
GRAHAM WINTER

A catalogue record for this book is available from the National Library of Australia

www.mindfulcricket.com

Winter, Graham (author)
Mindful Cricket: Workbook
ISBN (paperback) 978-1-922337-95-5
ISBN (eBook) 978-1-922337-32-0

Typeset Expo Serif 10/16
Internal images by Claire Magarey (*Somersault Design*)
Cover and book design by Green Hill Publishing

Mindful Cricket.

Contents

About The Author.

Graham Winter played First Class cricket before retiring early to pursue a career as a performance psychologist.

From winning Sheffield Shield and One Day Cup Teams, he stepped into a varied and high-profile career as the performance psychology coach to Olympic gold medallists, Test cricketers and the executive teams of international corporations.

Career highlights include: three times Chief Psychologist to the Australian Olympic Team, Consultant to the ICC Academy and Australian Test Cricket Team, Advisor/Designer with PwC's Asia Pacific Strategic Change practice, and Founder of consulting firm Think One Team Consulting (**www.thinkoneteam.com**).

Graham is the best-selling author of five books published by John Wiley, including *Think One Team*, *High Performance Leadership*, and *First Be Nimble*.

In *Mindful Cricket* he brings together his unique experiences and passion for performance psychology and cricket to challenge and equip cricketers and coaches to find better ways to play a sport which everyone knows is played above the shoulders.

Introduction.

If you have read *Mindful Cricket*, you will know this is not a Workbook about how to bowl or hit a cricket ball. A Workbook like that would teach you technical skills, which are important; but they're not what makes a successful cricketer.

Every outstanding cricketer understands that cricket is played above the shoulders. The mind is the secret to playing better cricket, yet cricket has a serious problem: our traditional approach to practising and playing the game leaves players ill-equipped to master the mental game of cricket. Mindful Cricket is a four-part framework which addresses that problem in a way that has the potential to change the way you think about cricket and how you practise and play the game.

This Workbook is designed to be used in three ways:

1

A Companion to the *Mindful Cricket* book
It is a practical guide to help readers of the *Mindful Cricket* book to immediately apply the Game Mindset principles and practices.

2

A Player's Introduction to Mindful Cricket and Game Mindset
Players who prefer a light introduction and plenty of activities and tools can immediately start working on their Game Mindset.

3

A Resource for Coaches
It is also a resource that coaches can provide to their players, to guide them through learning and applying Game Mindset as part of the overall cricket program.

Whichever group(s) you belong to, you'll be learning and applying a very practical framework with lots of tools and practices specifically designed for cricket.

To get the most from this book, I encourage you to take three actions:

1. Join the Mindful Cricket community at **www.mindfulcricket.com** so you have immediate access to the activities, guides and tools you'll need to apply the principles and practices;
2. Complete the Workbook activities, particularly the self-assessments and reflections;
3. Look for opportunities to apply your selected activities in cricket as well as in your day-to-day life, because this is the best way to learn and embed new habits.

I hope you enjoy using this Workbook and look forward to engaging with you through the website and Mindful Cricket community.

Note to Coaches

The *Mindful Cricket Workbook* is a resource to introduce Game Mindset to players at all levels from school and club to international. Enough detail is included from the *Mindful Cricket* book to lay the foundation understanding, and from there you can guide players to tackle the activities best suited to your program and their individual needs.

I recommend that you get your players to join the Mindful Cricket Community at **www.mindfulcricket.com,** where they will be able to access a growing range of tools and support.

Game Mindset Model.

Clear Mind.

Composed

Focused

Simple

Adapt fast

Play Brave.

Bold Vision

Put it on the Line

Hold the Tension

Play Clever.

Bat Smart

Bowl Smart

Keep & Field Smart

Play Better.

Growth Mindset

Be Game Ready

Bring Optimism

Part A.

THE GAME ABOVE THE SHOULDERS.

From an early age, we are told that cricket is played above the shoulders, which means the mind is the secret to playing better cricket. Technique and talent are not enough, yet the traditional approaches to practising and playing the game aren't designed to develop the mindset we need to be the best cricketers we can be.

Game Mindset offers a way to face down the mental challenges of the game and to develop skills and capabilities which have value well beyond just the cricket field. These are life skills which will equip you with a Clear Mind, and the mindset to Play Brave, Play Clever and Play Better.

CHAPTER 1

Why Is Technique Overrated?

The Difference Is Mindset.

Cricket is played above the shoulders. We all know this because we can play so well one day and then so poorly the next.

Our basic ability to bat, bowl, keep and field doesn't change. But form comes and goes like clouds on a windy day, so we do what cricketers have always done: we spend hours in the nets working on technique, timing and rhythm, only to end up even more frustrated when still playing poorly.

But what if the problem isn't technique or talent? What if the problem is the way we think about the game itself?

The Problem Is Simple.

Even the best players have flaws in their techniques - just look at Steve Smith or Jasprit Bumrah. Yet despite those flaws, they score runs and take wickets on a regular basis in all forms of the game.

Which players in world cricket seem to succeed despite being "unorthodox" in their game?

Technique and Talent Are Overrated.

Clear, confident, composed minds make runs and take wickets. Filling your mind with thoughts about technique or striving to get better won't help if you don't start with the right mindset.

Go to the nets with the wrong mindset and you'll grip the bat too tight, meet high catches with hard hands, and lose bowling rhythm by trying too hard.

What mindset do you take to the nets?

Mindfulness.

We play our best cricket (or do our best at anything) when we are mindful, which means our mind is clear, composed and fully focused on the challenges of the moment. However, we don't play so well when we are preoccupied with complicated thoughts or distracted by impatience, self-doubt or even over-confidence.

Many top athletes and teams around the world (from NBA stars, to Wimbledon champions and Olympic medallists) embrace mindfulness practices as an integral part of their training and development, as athletes and as people. Those practices develop the sort of patience and composure needed by cricketers. However, the big question is:

How can we make these mindful practices relevant and practical for cricketers
and cricket coaches so the benefits flow into our great game?

Game Mindset.

This question led me to create a four-step framework based on my personal experiences as a performance psychologist and First Class cricketer, to help cricketers and coaches find and develop this mindful approach in sport and life. I called the approach Game Mindset.

First Class players say that when they have learned and applied the Game Mindset approach, the game seems easier.

Game Mindset isn't complicated or contrived. Quite the opposite. It's a way of thinking and a suite of practices, activities, drills and tools built on mindfulness and performance psychology principles, designed to help you enjoy your cricket and be the best cricketer you can be.

Expectations.

What are the top three things you hope to gain from learning about Game Mindset and applying the principles and tools to your game? List them below.

The next chapter explores the challenges presented by the game of cricket. It reveals why cricket is definitely played above the shoulders and Game Mindset is so effective in helping cricketers to become the players they want to be.

CHAPTER 2

Why Cricket Is Played Above The Shoulders.

3 things you'll gain from this Chapter

1. Understand the mental demands of the game
2. Learn why mindset lets down batsmen and bowlers
3. Learn how to avoid mental errors

It's a Challenging Game.

Whether you are batting, bowling, fielding or keeping, mindset can make or break your performances. Let's explore the four key activities in cricket and why mindset makes the difference.

Mindful Batting.

Is there one aspect of the game more influenced by mindset than any other? If there is, it is likely to be batting. Here are three major reasons for that:

Instant Dismissal.

Even talented international players fear the dreaded "duck" and succumb to nerves early in their innings. Many bring a "don't get out'" mindset, which means they are worrying about what they don't want, and not surprisingly they tighten their grip on the bat, move tentatively and create the very conditions where their greatest fear is more likely to come true. Mindful Cricket helps to get through the fear of failure by cultivating composure and focusing on what's important to build an innings.

Position in Batting Order.

Facing new ball bowlers requires quick reactions, good judgement of line and length, and courage. Middle order challenges are many and varied so adaptability is vital; and the lower order often score the runs that make the difference between winning and losing, so concentration is essential.

Adapting to Conditions.

Cricket is played in different formats, on a wide range of pitches and using a ball that changes as an innings progresses. And, of course, the opposition bowlers, fielders and captain all bring challenges to which batsmen must adapt.

Reflection Questions

At the start of the innings are you usually positive in intent or more focused on avoiding being dismissed?

Do feelings like nervousness and frustration ever hinder your decision making?

Do you have simple and repeatable ways to reset your concentration when distracted?

What improvement in mindset would have the biggest positive impact on your batting?

Mindful Bowling.

Here are some reasons why mindset plays a key part in bowling:

Physical Demands.

Fatigued bowlers lose their line and length. Long spells, hot or cold conditions, and bowling into strong winds all play a part; and then there are the short form matches, where bowling single overs in separate spells means being physically and mentally ready from the first ball.

It's Not Fair.

The laws of the game are heavily weighted in the batsman's favour - benefit of the doubt, no leg side LBWs, ropes for shorter boundaries, and so on. Your best ball can be hit for six, or the pitch can be so flat that even the most perfect leg break doesn't catch the edge of the bat. The keys to success as a bowler are persistence and patience.

Strategy and Tactics.

Mindful Bowling is not expecting a wicket every ball. Small rewards come from shaping the way the batsman plays, and by using all types of variations in line, length, pace and movement to create the false stroke. Creating and executing clever strategies and tactics is fundamental to bowling success.

Reflection Questions

Do you enjoy the challenge of working out a batsman's weaknesses, or do you just go all out for a wicket every ball?

Can you keep composure and rhythm when the batsmen are in control?

Do you have a simple and repeatable bowling routine?

How many wickets are you missing out on because you lose belief and control when things aren't going well?

Mindful Wicket-Keeping.

Wicket-keepers play a vital team role not just in taking catches and making stumpings, but also in setting standards, energy and tempo in the field.

The mental challenges of keeping are a mix of those for batting and bowling; plus a few that are specific to being behind the stumps.

Physical Demands.

Keepers are on the field for the whole innings, so the demands on endurance, flexibility and quick running to get to the stumps for run out opportunities are high.

Ball-By-Ball Concentration.

Keepers focus when the bowler runs in, and remain fully alert until the ball has been played and is dead. We take it for granted that they will pick the spinner's wrong 'un, stop wide balls down the leg side, pick up the low catches that fall in front of the slips, and sprint to the stumps whenever a run is taken.

Balance, Movement and Timing.

Keeping has high points, like taking a diving catch, and low points, such as missing an easy stumping. All of these are affected by the keepers' balance, movement and timing. Amongst these, attention to footwork and glovework are key.

Keeper Batsman.

The outstanding success of wicket-keeper batsmen like Kumar Sangakkara and Alyssa Healy has transformed the expectations, roles and skills of wicket-keepers. In fact, many First Class teams have two or three batsmen who are all competent keepers.

> **Reflection Questions**
>
> How well equipped are you to meet the physical demands of keeping?
>
> What are your strengths and opportunities for improvement in concentration?
>
> How are your footwork and glovework? Are there strengths to leverage and areas to develop?
>
> How much contribution do you want to make with the bat?

Mindful Fielding.

A team of average bowlers supported by energetic fielders, who grab half chances and excel in ground fielding, can pressure strong batting sides and create opportunities which turn matches. On the flip side, dropping catches and giving away easy runs can demoralise bowlers and make it so much more difficult to win. Mindset is important to making the most of your abilities in this essential part of the game.

Motivation in the Field.

Poor fielders bring little energy or attention; but the best fielders have a positive attitude, do lots of practice, and know how to switch concentration on and off. They set themselves high standards on the field and want the ball to be hit to them.

Ball-By-Ball Concentration.

The ability to switch concentration on and off has a lot to do with routines or rituals. Some players like to chat between deliveries, and others will walk back to the marked spot and then move in quickly as the bowler begins their run. The key is to be alert for catches, and opportunities to impact the play by cutting off runs or creating run outs.

Confidence.

Everyone drops catches, but for some fielders it shatters their confidence. If it happens to you, put it behind you and get on with making the most of the next opportunity.

Reflection Questions

What mindset do you bring to your fielding?

How effectively do you switch your concentration on and off in the field?

How do you react to dropping a catch or misfielding?

What would increase your positive impact in the field?

Chapter Takeaways.

Mindful Cricket begins with understanding the challenges of the game and the role of mindset in successfully meeting these challenges. How you handle feelings, focus and self-belief is likely to make or break the enjoyment and results you get from cricket.

Jot down your insights from this Chapter:

Quotes from the *Mindful Cricket* book:

Nervousness and frustration derail batsmen, along with the fear of failure and loss of focus on what's happening in the moment. Mindful Practices can build calmness, composure and concentration to take it on one ball at a time.

. . . .

Too much tension destroys rhythm, which causes bowlers to lose their line, length and "zip", just as fatigue and distraction take away energy. Mindful Practices help bowlers to create opportunities by sticking to their plans, and absorbing and applying pressure.

. . . .

Wicket-keeping and fielding each have their own challenges and requirements for a mindset of focus, energy and teamwork.

. . . .

Cricket has many unique challenges, which mindful players accept and enjoy. That is why they are successful in playing the game above the shoulders.

. . . .

CHAPTER 3

Mindset To The Rescue.

3 things you'll gain from this Chapter

1. Recognise the four enemies of a Clear Mind
2. Assess the clarity of your mind in moments that matter
3. Learn why Game Mindset defeats the enemies of a Clear Mind

Enemies of a Clear Mind.

This brief chapter highlights four "enemies" which make cricket seem a lot more difficult than it needs to be, and shows why developing your own unique Game Mindset can be so powerful.

1. A Reactive Mind.

The first enemy is letting your mind become so reactive that you lose composure and let unhelpful and uncomfortable emotions take over. Without composure, bowlers lose rhythm, batsmen lose judgement and fielders lose touch. Mistimed shots, erratic bowling and dropped catches are rarely caused by poor technique or talent, but rather by loss of composure.

> Do you maintain poise and composure in the moments that matter, or do you let uncomfortable feelings like nervousness and frustration take over?

2. Distraction and Mind Drift.

Without focus in the present when batting, you will miss cues from bowlers and fail to really watch the ball; and when you are bowling, your consistency of line and length will likely suffer. Poor umpiring decisions, playing and missing, dropping a catch, or worrying about winning or losing can all create mind drift away from here and now and put your performance at risk.

Is staying focused in the moment easy for you, or does your mind drift to what happened the ball before or what might happen in the future?

3. Making It Complicated.

The third enemy is making it complicated rather than Keeping It Simple. With the best of intentions, we overthink by trying to control all that's happening. When we make things too complicated, we lose trust in our game and try too hard, rather than letting our well-practised skills and instincts take over.

Do you naturally keep things simple and uncomplicated, or do you tend to overthink or get a scrambled mind when there's a lot happening?

4. Slow to Change.

The fourth enemy is being slow and inflexible in adapting to the changes. You can't play cricket successfully without the ability to adapt to the conditions and the game itself. Cricket is constantly changing. No two pitches are the same, all bowlers are different, and even balls that look the same behave differently.

How quickly can you adapt to different pitches and forms of the game, and to the rapidly shifting tactics that emerge during a match?

....

If any of these enemies seem familiar, that's entirely expected because they are universal enemies to which we are all susceptible. The good news is you can learn to do something about it.

....

A Simple Formula.

Are you frustrated, or optimistic that there's more to your game - more runs, wickets, catches and fun?

Things can be different. Things can be better. For this to happen consistently, you need a formula - a simple, reliable formula which clears the mind of the four enemies, embraces the challenge and helps you to master the game in even the toughest of circumstances

That formula is **your unique Game Mindset**. Let's identify, develop and hone it so you can play Mindful Cricket.

Chapter Takeaways.

Everyone confronts four enemies in batting, bowling, keeping, fielding, and in our general lives, which can make almost anything seem complicated and overwhelming. These enemies are a reactive mind, distraction and mind drift, making it complicated, and being slow to adapt. A Game Mindset defeats these enemies.

Jot down your insights from this Chapter:

Quotes from the *Mindful Cricket* book:

On the flipside of the four enemies sits a brilliantly clear insight: we play better when
Composed, Focused In the Moment, Keeping It Simple, and Adapting Fast.

....

When the ball is delivered, clear-minded batsmen are still,
poised, focused in the moment and ready to adapt.

....

Clear-minded bowlers stick to their routines and rituals, and their rhythms and
plans, without letting a lucky shot upset their focus and confidence.

....

Clear-minded captains make the right calls; clear-minded keepers and fielders catch with
soft hands and throw down stumps; and clear-minded umpires make accurate decisions.

....

Part B.

INTRODUCING THE GAME MINDSET.

Cricket is a game of differing tempos and varying intensities, so when you really understand how to create your own Game Mindset you can relax, and trust your technique and talent to produce better results in all types of conditions.

Teammates and opponents will see this in the way you "**own your space**", which means projecting a sense of balance and calm in your basic set-up. It will show in the little rituals for each delivery and in how you do things at a pace and in a way that suits you over and over again. While other players look rushed and disorganised when batting, bowling, keeping or fielding, you are balanced and in control.

Game Mindset will also show in the way you **"hold your shape"**. You might already recognise what happens when players lose their shape. Batsmen get out of balance, perhaps pushing too hard at the ball or getting outside their natural range of strokes; bowlers overstride or fall away in the follow-through; and keepers get untidy in their footwork and glovework. The opposite is easy to see.

A player with a Game Mindset looks in control because they own their space and hold their shape. That's Mindful Cricket, and you can unlock its power and simplicity by learning to develop your own unique Game Mindset.

Game Mindset Model.

Clear Mind.

Composed

Focused

Simple

Adapt fast

Play Brave.

Bold Vision

Put it on the Line

Hold the Tension

Play Clever.

Bat Smart

Bowl Smart

Keep & Field Smart

Play Better.

Growth Mindset

Be Game Ready

Bring Optimism

CHAPTER 4

The Game Mindset Framework.

1. Understand the Pillars and principles of Game Mindset
2. Self-assess your current capabilities and practices
3. Identify initial priorities for improvement

The Four Pillars.

Here is the mindset of nearly every cricketer who has consistently mastered his or her game in Tests, First Class, club, school or courtyard cricket:

CLEAR MIND	Composed, focused, keeping it simple and adapting fast
PLAY BRAVE	Bold vision, putting it on the line, and holding the tension
PLAY CLEVER	Bringing cricket smarts to their game
PLAY BETTER	Applying a growth mindset, being game ready and optimistic.

That's it. And you'll see elements of this mindset in batsmen, bowlers, keepers and fielders in every game you watch from now on.

Let's now review each Pillar and the foundation principles of Game Mindset, then you will self-assess your current capabilities and identify initial priorities for development (for which you can find the resources in this Workbook, the *Mindful Cricket* book and at **www.mindfulcricket.com**).

PILLAR 1: Clear Mind.

A Clear Mind is composed and focused in the moment, has simple plans and adapts in an instant. This lays the foundation for all aspects of Game Mindset, because clarity is the key to being the best you can be. And creating a Clear Mind isn't just valuable for your cricket, it is absolutely a life skill with benefits for study, career and family life.

Four Principles for Creating a Clear Mind.

1. **Cultivate Composure.** Composure is many things. It's calmness and poise in tense moments, it's patience to deal with frustrations and setbacks, and it's accepting the ups and downs of cricket and life.

2. **Focus In The Moment.** Minds go to what interests them, which means we're often not giving full attention to the moment. At the heart of mindfulness is the skill to patiently bring your distracted mind back to the present, which is the only place where you can take wickets or score runs.

3. **Keep It Simple.** Simplicity is knowing and doing the Basics, playing to your strengths and applying pressure to opponents. "Simple" consistently delivers under pressure; complicated doesn't.

4. **Adapt Fast.** Adaptability is the key to playing in unpredictable and fast changing conditions. It's thinking on your feet and using "learning loops" to Plan, Do, Check and Adapt.

Self-Assessment.

Instructions:

Reflect on how much you agree or disagree that the statements below apply to your cricket game. Use the five-point scale to rate each item and then complete the analysis section below.

1 Strongly Disagree **2** Disagree **3** Neither Agree Nor Disagree **4** Agree **5** Strongly Agree

	1	2	3	4	5
Composure					
Calm and poised in tense moments					
Patient when faced with frustrations and setbacks					
Accepting of the ups and downs of cricket and life					
Focus in the Moment					
Stay focused on one ball at a time when batting					
Reset concentration when distracted					
Sustain concentration when bowling, keeping or fielding					
Keep it Simple					
Do the Basics under pressure					
Keep a clear and uncluttered mind					
Put pressure back on opponents					

Adapt Fast	1	2	3	4	5
Adapt quickly to new conditions	○	○	○	○	○
Think on your feet as situations unfold	○	○	○	○	○
Agile in applying new tactics and strategies	○	○	○	○	○

Analysis.

Reflect on your scores on individual items and consider which areas are a potential priority.

Strengths to Leverage
(Scores of 5)

Development Opportunities
(Scores of 3-4)

Potential Derailers
(Scores of 1-2)

PILLAR 2: Play Brave.

Sport psychologists have found the advantage lies with the bold and decisive athlete, the one who goes towards the challenge and knows and trusts their abilities.

Play Brave isn't about recklessly swinging at every ball, tossing up inviting leg breaks, or bouncing the best opposition batsman relentlessly. Sometimes it's brave to play with restraint and not bowl your best delivery until the batsman is looking comfortable. It takes courage to defend the good deliveries in a 20/20 game, knowing you'll take responsibility to guide the team home later.

Three Principles of Play Brave.

1. **Create Your Bold Vision**. Bold cricket is aiming towards your goals, projecting positive body language, seeking small victories and believing good things will happen in even the toughest of circumstances.

2. **Put It On The Line**. Putting It On the Line is being willing to take risks to go for what you want to achieve. It can mean risking the quick single to give your teammate the strike, playing the bold shot, or saying what no one else will say at the team meeting because you know it needs to be said.

3. **Hold The Tension**. This is about persisting when things aren't easy and continuing to apply pressure when results aren't coming. It's resisting the temptation to try for a wicket ball late in an over, or not giving up your wicket with a wild shot.

Self-Assessment.

Instructions:

Reflect on how much you agree or disagree that the statements below apply to your cricket game. Use the five-point scale to rate each item and then complete the analysis section below.

1 Strongly Disagree   **2** Disagree   **3** Neither Agree Nor Disagree   **4** Agree   **5** Strongly Agree

Bold Vision	1	2	3	4	5
Have bold aspirations that really motivate you	○	○	○	○	○
Have clear, challenging but attainable mid-term goals	○	○	○	○	○
Have action plans to meet the goals	○	○	○	○	○

Put It On The Line	1	2	3	4	5
Tend to go towards success rather than avoid failure	○	○	○	○	○
Reliably apply the Basics in moments that matter	○	○	○	○	○
Willing to take risks, make mistakes and learn	○	○	○	○	○

Hold The Tension	1	2	3	4	5
Act with patience and good judgement in key moments	○	○	○	○	○
Understand and positively shape the momentum of matches	○	○	○	○	○
Show persistence when things get tough	○	○	○	○	○

Analysis.

Reflect on your scores on individual items and consider which areas are a potential priority.

Strengths to Leverage
(Scores of 5)

Development Opportunities
(Scores of 3-4)

Potential Derailers
(Scores of 1-2)

PILLAR 3: Play Clever.

There is a big difference between clever cricket and dumb cricket. Clever cricketers know their game and bring match awareness. This means they are skilled at reading the game and making good decisions, which play a vital part in shaping the momentum.

Three Principles to Play Clever.

1. **Bat Smart.** This is about building trust in your batting Basics, such as holding your shape under pressure, learning to adapt to change, building partnerships and applying and absorbing pressure.
2. **Bowl Smart.** This means learning how to read the game and bringing smart and subtle variations to shift momentum. It's also about knowing your game, working in bowling partnerships and adapting to change.
3. **Keep and Field Smart.** Keepers play a vital role in setting and maintaining standards in the field, and in supporting captains and bowlers to apply pressure. When keepers and fielders bring a Game Mindset, they make even an average bowling attack look awesome.

Self-Assessment.

Instructions:

Reflect on how much you agree or disagree that the statements below apply to your cricket game. Use the five-point scale to rate each item and then complete the analysis section below.

1 Strongly Disagree   **2** Disagree   **3** Neither Agree Nor Disagree   **4** Agree   **5** Strongly Agree

	1	2	3	4	5
Bat Smart					
Have trust in doing the batting Basics well in all situations	○	○	○	○	○
Contribute to batting partnerships	○	○	○	○	○
Absorb and Apply Pressure when batting	○	○	○	○	○
Bowl Smart					
Have trust in doing the bowling Basics well in all situations	○	○	○	○	○
Play your role in bowling partnerships	○	○	○	○	○
Absorb and Apply Pressure when bowling	○	○	○	○	○
Keep and Field Smart					
Do the fielding Basics well in all situations	○	○	○	○	○
Contribute to the team effort in the field	○	○	○	○	○
Bring a positive mindset onto the field	○	○	○	○	○

Analysis.

Reflect on your scores on individual items and consider which areas are a potential priority.

Strengths to Leverage
(Scores of 5)

Development Opportunities
(Scores of 3-4)

Potential Derailers
(Scores of 1-2)

PILLAR 4: Play Better.

The best athletes across all sports display a Growth Mindset (Carol Dweck, 2008), which means they believe their most basic abilities can be developed through dedication and hard work, despite the belief of many that talent is fixed. They also prepare extremely well to be "game ready" and tend to be more optimistic than pessimistic. Accordingly, they are constantly seeking ways to Play Better.

Three Principles to Play Better.

1. **Apply a Growth Mindset**. Three Growth Mindset strategies are commonly employed by high performers: taking a strengths-first approach, finding and accepting feedback, and taking care of yourself. These set up the basic mindset for learning and developing.
2. **Be Game Ready.** Awareness of what makes you think and feel at your best, and the daily habits to consistently make that happen are the foundation for clever cricket. Then it's about using these insights to create your pre-game and pre-performance routines and rituals.
3. **Bring Optimism.** We see the world differently depending on whether our "mindset filter" is optimistic or pessimistic. Developing your optimistic filter means learning and applying a way of thinking which reduces anxiety and improves confidence and outcomes.

Self-Assessment.

Instructions:

Reflect on how much you agree or disagree that the statements below apply to your cricket game. Use the five-point scale to rate each item and then complete the analysis section below.

1 Strongly Disagree **2** Disagree **3** Neither Agree Nor Disagree **4** Agree **5** Strongly Agree

Apply a Growth Mindset

	1	2	3	4	5
Believe improvement comes from work not just talent	○	○	○	○	○
Openly seek and receive feedback even if it stings a bit	○	○	○	○	○
Take good care of physical and mental wellbeing	○	○	○	○	○

Game Readiness

	1	2	3	4	5
Have good daily habits and disciplines	○	○	○	○	○
Know how to prepare to play	○	○	○	○	○
Consistently apply pre-game routines and rituals	○	○	○	○	○

Bring Optimism

	1	2	3	4	5
Confront difficult situations with an optimistic mindset	○	○	○	○	○
Use positive words and language when thinking and talking	○	○	○	○	○
Feel grateful for the positive things in life	○	○	○	○	○

Analysis.

Reflect on your scores on individual items and consider which areas are a potential priority.

Strengths to Leverage (Scores of 5)	
Development Opportunities (Scores of 3-4)	
Potential Derailers (Scores of 1-2)	

Game Mindset - A Stance for the Mind.

You couldn't imagine a batsman without a stance. The stance is the framework onto which everything else is attached. A good stance is balanced, simple and gets the batsman ready to play the ball.

Game Mindset is like the batting stance. It's simple, balanced and gets you game ready. It is unique and personal to you and it is the key to playing Mindful Cricket.

The next chapter explores the mindset you bring to cricket and will help you to discover the unique triggers for you to be at your best. From that foundation, the following four sections take you step-by-step through how to create the Game Mindset you need to be the best cricketer you can be.

Chapter Takeaways.

Mindful Cricket is about one thing that powers a thousand other things: mindset. No one masters this game with the wrong mindset, and everyone can play better with a Game Mindset.

Mindset is the beliefs, thoughts, attitudes and habits you bring to the game. It is the most important tool you have because it can make every other aspect of your game better.

What have your learned about your mindset and how it affects your cricket?

Quotes from the *Mindful Cricket* book:

Game Mindset is poised and confident, whereas the alternative invariably showcases the four enemies: a reactive mind, distraction, making it complicated and being slow to change.

....

To better understand Game Mindset, reflect for a moment on how mindset shows in the way a player "owns" the space around them, and in the physical "shape" of their game.

....

Game Mindset is like the batting stance. It's simple, balanced and gets you game ready. It is the key to playing Mindful Cricket.

....

When you really understand how to create your own Game Mindset, you can relax and trust your technique and talent to produce better results in many different settings.

....

CHAPTER 5

Discover Your Unique Game Mindset.

It's the Zone You Want.

Have you heard a cricketer, tennis player or footballer say they were "in the zone"? Chances are they were talking about the mindset of being totally focused on the game, with all the energy, rhythm and confidence flowing in the right way - it was almost effortless and yet so good!

> Have you had that experience of batting or bowling almost effortlessly - bowling with rhythm and natural control of line, length and variation, and batting with such confidence you see the ball early and clearly, let it come to you, and strike it easily through the gaps in the field?

How the Zone Reveals Your Unique Game Mindset.

Imagine a cricket match is about to begin. You jog onto the field with your teammates and then stand back for a moment to observe what's happening.

Some are running and tossing the ball to sharpen their reflexes; the opening bowlers are pacing their run-ups; and others are stretching and looking at the sky, adjusting their eyes to the surroundings. The opposition openers are approaching the pitch.

Imagine you can see the mindset of each of your teammates and opponents in the colour of their cap or helmet:

- **Blue Caps** are in the mindset to achieve. They're active, sharp, energetic and confident. They feel in control of their game and are looking forward to getting into the contest. They're ready to take a sharp catch, to bowl with energy and rhythm, or to play each ball on its merits.
- **Red Caps** are in the mindset to attack. They're more hyped or psyched than the blue caps. They might be feeling too nervous or impatient. They're more likely to be impulsive. You'll see it in bowlers running in faster and being very aggressive, or in the batters getting frustrated and playing high-risk shots. They might succeed but the percentages aren't good over the long term.
- **Orange Caps** are in the mindset to avoid. They haven't brought the right energy, which might be because they're tired or bored, or they're preoccupied with fear, doubt and worry. They don't have their usual zip as bowlers, they're slow to respond in the field, and as batters they look tentative.

The caps are "mind zones." Blue cap, or Blue Zone, is where we play our most consistent cricket. Red and Orange Zones don't mean you won't do well, just that you have a lower percentage chance of success.

Reflection Questions

What coloured "mind cap" do you usually wear onto the field?

What makes it change colour?

How much of your cricket success and enjoyment comes down to wearing the right mind cap?

How valuable will it be to learn ways to get that blue cap on more often?

ACTIVITY: Finding Your Performance Zone.

This activity applies five tools to help create Blue Zone experiences, and shows why Game Mindset is the key to Mindful Cricket.

To make the most of this activity, download the Guide and Toolsheets from **www.mindfulcricket.com**.

ZONE TOOL 1: Understanding Your Performance Zones.

WHAT'S YOUR BLUE ZONE?

How do you think when you are in that Blue Zone? (eg clear mind, quick and clear decisions)

How does being in the Blue Zone change the way you feel? (eg composed, energetic)

What do you do better as a cricketer when you are in the Blue Zone? (eg judge line and length, rhythm and timing)

WHAT'S YOUR RED ZONE?

How do you think when you are in that Red Zone? (eg rushed, unclear)

How does being in the Red Zone change the way you feel? (eg impatient, aggressive)

How does the Red Zone change the way you play? (eg lose my shape, take more risks)

WHAT'S YOUR ORANGE ZONE?

How do you think when you are
in that Orange Zone? (eg preoccupied,
avoiding mistakes)

How does being in the Orange Zone
change the way you feel? (eg more
worried and self-doubting)

How does the Orange Zone change the
way you play? (eg
tentative shots, slower to react)

ZONE TOOL 2: Capture Insights for Action.

The Player's Journal note below is a recent example of the insights to be gained by getting to know your performance zones.

PLAYERS JOURNAL

The Blue Zone activity helped me recognise how often I've been pushing myself into the Red. When I look back on the last few months, I can see I've lost composure and confidence and become more impatient and easily frustrated. That's not my Game Mindset – so I've got something to work on now which feels simple and about my game.

Use the Reflection Questions which follow to jot down any insights you've gained about the differences in mindset between the three zones and how this has been affecting your enjoyment and performance of the game.

Reflection Questions

What do you see as the key difference between your mindset in the three zones (eg clarity of thinking)?
How does each zone affect your performance and enjoyment?
Can you recognise these zones in other aspects of your life (eg work, study)?

ZONE TOOL 3: How to Find Your Zone Triggers and Blockers.

Triggering your Blue Zone isn't like the law of gravity - it doesn't always work. However, there are many Mindful Cricket practices to help make it more consistent. There are at least six ways to trigger the Blue Zone, and they are outlined below with questions to help you unpack how they apply to your game.

1. Find a Challenge.

What activities and challenges trigger your Blue Zone?

2. Set Clear, Meaningful Goals.

What goals or which purpose seem to bring out your best?

3. Stretch Yourself.

When you "size" a challenge and feel it's achievable at a stretch, that is usually a great motivator. What are stretch challenges for you?

4. Clear Your Mind.

What physical or mental preparation helps you to bring a Clear Mind to practice and games?

5. Focus Intently on the Challenges at Hand.

How effectively do you stay in the present moment? What causes mind drift? What helps you to set aside thoughts about what has happened or might happen, and to refocus on the present moment?

6. Open Up to Feedback.

What's your mindset towards feedback from coaches and teammates? How do mistakes and setbacks seem different when you are in the different zones?

Take a few moments to reflect on your answers to the questions in each of these six trigger areas, so you have the ammunition needed to create your Blue Zone Plan.

ZONE TOOL 4: Create Your Blue Zone Plan.

Here are three questions in Stop–Start–Continue format, to help you begin drafting your Blue Zone Plan:

Stop or Do Less

What will you stop or do less to get more time in Blue and less in Red or Orange?
(eg rushing preparation and being reactive to what other people say or do)

Start or Do More

What will you start or do more to get more time in Blue and less in Red or Orange?
(eg use the Game Mindset tools to be composed and game ready)

Continue

What habits, rituals and actions will you keep doing to create Blue Zone experiences?
(eg stay with pre-game routines, and bowling cues)

The Create Your Blue Zone Plan activity is intended to get you more familiar with your performance zones and to understand how much you influence that in your preparation and mindset.

ZONE TOOL 5: Debrief Your Zone Performances.

The best way to get more Blue Zone experiences is to be aware of what triggers or blocks them, and then build those into your Game Readiness plans. You can do that by debriefing your match experiences.

Here's an example drawn from a Scenario in the *Mindful Cricket* book:

Zones I experienced during the match...	*How that affected my behaviours...*
Too much Red Zone when starting my innings and when under pressure to score runs. Really nervous at the start of my innings and felt pressure to keep the score moving.	Started off tentatively, then took unnecessary risks and lost control of the shot by lifting my head and trying to overhit it.

What triggered those zones...	*What to stop, start or continue...*
Poor rushed routine before batting, too much focus on score and doubting my own ability to pace the innings.	Have all my gear ready when a wicket falls. Plan with my batting partner – don't just take it on myself. Be calmer and more confident.

Zone Debriefing Questions.

After each match, use these four questions to learn and adapt. Try this now by reflecting on your most recent experiences.

1. What zones did you experience?

2. How did that change your behaviours?

3. What triggered those zones (eg was it preparation or in-the-game experiences)?

4. What can you stop, start or continue to get more in the Blue Zone?

Practice Tip: Debriefing is an important practice to build into your rituals and routines because it drives the all-important feedback and learning which are essential to Playing Better.

Chapter Takeaways.

The Zone is an ideal place to understand what Game Mindset means and to discover your own unique mindset. The core to that mindset is the Blue Zone, in which you feel more in control of your game, and that means a clearer mind, bolder decision making, clever thinking and openness to learn and play better.

Jot down your insights from this Chapter:

Quotes from the *Mindful Cricket* book:

Mindful Cricket is composed, focused in the present moment (when needed), and uncomplicated. This way of thinking is developed through Game Mindset practices.

....

Mindful Cricket is continually learning and refining ways to trigger the Blue Zone.

....

Understanding what is unique about your Game Mindset will set you up to choose and apply Mindful Cricket principles and practices in ways that best suit you.

....

Part C.

GAME MINDSET - THE FOUR PILLARS.

Here's a simple 4-point checklist to use in any match situation to reflect on your current mindset:

Clear Mind – composed, focused, and keeping it simple?

Play Brave - looking for ways to succeed (not to avoid failure)?

Play Clever - reading the game and making smart choices?

Play Better – well prepared and open to learn?

This part of the book is the deep dive into the principles, practices, activities and tools to help you develop the Game Mindset to be the best cricketer you can be.

Pillar 1.
Clear Mind

PILLAR 1: Clear Mind.

You want to be your best, enjoy the game and achieve success, but somewhere in amongst the expectations and pressures you lose focus on what matters and make it harder to succeed. Frustration builds, confidence drops, and you make complicated plans for what is essentially a simple game.

You can quieten the noise, reduce the clutter and take the weight off yourself. It starts with awareness of the Blue Zone, and then strengthening your ability to bring a Clear Mind by applying four core principles of Mindful Cricket:

- Cultivate Composure
- Focus In The Moment
- Keep It Simple
- Adapt Fast.

These principles are laid out over the next four chapters. The order in which they are introduced is important, because composure and focus are the two foundation mindfulness principles and practices which take on the enemies of reactive mind and distraction.

With those foundations in place, you'll be ready to Keep It Simple and Learn and Adapt Fast to the changing conditions of cricket matches.

CHAPTER 6

Cultivate Composure.

3 things you'll gain from this Chapter

1. Be more accepting of your own emotions
2. Learn to develop calmness and composure
3. Quieten your inner critic

Cricket Composure.

Composure is many things: it's the calmness and courage to hold your shape against the fastest bowler you've ever faced; it's the patience to stick with your plan when your mind wants to give it up; and it's accepting the poor umpiring decision and getting on with the next delivery.

Above all, composure is not the absence of emotions. Composed players still feel anxious, frustrated and deflated; but they've trained themselves to project positive body language while letting the uncomfortable feelings roll through with no more attention than they deserve. Composure in moments that matter is the foundation for a reliable Game Mindset.

Reflection Questions

When are the "moments that matter" for you?

Do you bring calmness and composure to those moments?

What benefits would you gain, in cricket and in life, by developing greater composure?

Two Villains Disrupt Composure.

Two "big" villains, called *The Inner Critic* and *The Noisy Mind*, create a reactive mind instead of calmness and composure.

The Inner Critic.

Early in our cricket careers we learn to grip the bat, get our head in line with the ball, catch with soft hands and move through the crease when bowling. However, with few exceptions, we never learn how to quieten the inner critic who points out our limitations and mistakes, and creates all manner of fears and worries, most of which never happen.

To build composure, we need to quieten our inner critic and instead learn to deal with someone more reasonable and positive.

> Do you have an inner critic? How does it affect your cricket?

The Noisy Mind.

Does day-to-day life train your mind to focus calmly and intently on one thing and do it well, or does it encourage you to be constantly thinking of something in the past or speculating about the future?

If, like most players, you have a hectic life, then beware of the Red Zone coming into play!

To enter a match composed and focused means slowing down and quietening your mind so you aren't overreacting to what's happening.

> Do you have times when your mind is noisy and rushed when you need it to be calm and composed?

You can build three lines of defence against these villains, by employing Mindful Practices to create composure as the centrepiece of your Game Mindset.

MINDFUL PRACTICE 1: Accept Your Emotions.

When we head into the "battle" of competition, our minds and bodies change. There are at least seven signs that your body is telling you it's getting ready to perform:

Signs You Are Getting Ready to Perform

Faster breathing	Dry mouth	Tense muscles
Pounding heart	Queasy stomach	Need to urinate
	Dizziness	

These are reflexes. They are valuable, short-lived, and (with a sensible inner critic) they are all signs that you are good to go. However, for many players these aren't signs of readiness, but something to fear and avoid. Does that sound familiar for you?

WHY EMOTIONS ARE YOUR FRIEND.

Your ancestors survived tigers, hostile tribes and all manner of life-threatening situations because anxiety and fear motivated them to avoid risks, or be ready to fight and win if needed. That means you have inherited a finely tuned radar which loves to pick up and exaggerate threats.

That radar is very helpful for surviving tigers, but in a modern world the tigers are mostly in our minds, so we end up anxious, frustrated or angry when we'd rather be excited, composed and ready to play.

Use the Reflection Questions below to begin leaning into the uncomfortable feelings rather than avoiding them or seeing them as negative. Take time to consider whether you need to be concerned about the nervous and anxious feelings, or whether they are just the same feelings that kept your ancestors safe for thousands of years.

Reflection Questions

What pre-game nerves or other uncomfortable feelings do you experience?

Do they affect your confidence and focus?

What would be different if you leaned in and welcomed these emotions by accepting and embracing the uncomfortable feelings?

What's important to do differently when you think about feelings?

Practice Tip: Build composure by accepting that uncomfortable feelings are okay, and that they can in fact be extremely helpful, provided you don't interpret the feeling of adrenaline and extra blood pumping through your body as anything other than a natural response designed to get you game ready.

Moods and Emotions.

An important point here is the difference between temporary emotions and moods: moods last for a longer time than emotions. If you are concerned about moods such as being anxious or depressed, then it's time to chat about it with your doctor or a counsellor or coach; they'll be able to help you understand what's happening and how best to handle those concerns. One thing we do know about evolutionary emotions is that feelings help us to understand each other better; it's not only perfectly natural to talk about emotions, it's an important way to break patterns of thinking which can be unhelpful if we keep them to ourselves.

MINDFUL PRACTICE 2: Find Your Calm Centre.

The foundation skills for building calmness and composure in moments that matter are to train yourself to:

1. Find the stillness or "calm centre" within your own mind and body
2. Bring attention back into the present moment.

....

These are amongst the most powerful Mindful Practices for enhancing wellbeing and performance, because they reduce the power of those uncomfortable feelings.

....

ACTIVITY 1: Clear Your Mind – Begin with Stillness.

The idea of stillness seems almost out of place in a world where things are happening all the time. There's always something to focus on or do, and that sets up a reactive mindset and creates an expectation to always be switched on.

The intention of this activity is to slow everything down and to see what mental and physical stillness feels like. Research and countless reports from athletes show that this very simple activity can have a profound effect on composure, if you are open to experiencing it and practising the steps that follow.

Find a quiet place where you can sit comfortably without distraction for 10 minutes.

Here is the outline of a script which you can listen to at **www.mindfulcricket.com:**

Settle into a comfortable, well balanced position on your chair with your feet flat on the floor, and your hands in your lap.

Choose whether you'd prefer to close your eyes, or to lower your gaze and keep them open.

For the next ten minutes do nothing but sit relaxed and still, and just observe what that feels like.

Don't try to force your thinking onto anything in particular. If you become aware that your mind has wandered, just bring your attention back to your breathing as a point for your concentration.

Just be still and observe what's happening in your mind and body.

Give it a go and then try the questions below.

Reflection Questions

How did it feel to just sit and do nothing?

What did you notice about your attention during this exercise?

Did you, like most people, find that your mind wandered?

Is it possible that your mind always wanders like this when playing cricket?

Stillness is such a simple yet powerful practice, which directly contributes to having a Clear Mind. Athletes like Formula One drivers quieten their minds before competition. They know the adrenaline will kick in and get them up when the race is about to begin, so they sit quietly and find that stillness inside themselves.

Practice Tip: Take 10 minutes each day to just sit quietly, and when your mind wanders just bring it back without judgement to your breathing. You will be training your mind to come into the moment when you need it most.

ACTIVITY 2: Centred Breathing for Composure.

The use of breathing or the breath as a trigger for calmness and focus is a foundation for many advanced Mindful Practices. It seems almost too simple, but this brief Player's Journal Report from the *Mindful Cricket* book describes the benefits:

PLAYER'S JOURNAL

Breathing is the key to my mental game because it's so natural and gives me three real advantages. As a daily ritual it calms me down so I'm less reactive than I used to be in sport and work. In games I use it to bring back composure, and it's also part of my set-up every delivery. My Psych told me that every emotion has a different breathing pattern and that made me realise I could tap back the other way and build calmness and composure. Every cricketer should do a mindful breathing course - the benefits are excellent.

Breath is incredibly powerful as a tool to guide your focus and control your emotions. Not only does it have direct connection to your emotions but it's something you can access at any time; and as you'll see later, it's a key part of the practices which boost concentration in the heat of competition. Developing the skill of Centred Breathing is a powerful foundation for your Game Mindset.

Here is the outline for a script (available in audio form at **www.mindfulcricket.com**) which I strongly encourage you to practise at home for 10-20 minutes every day, on a daily basis:

Centred Breathing Script Instructions:

Allocate at least 10 minutes to this activity, which is best done in a place where you won't be disrupted by people or devices.

Take the same seated stance as you did for the Stillness Activity. Feet flat on the floor, hands in your lap, and begin relaxing as you draw the breath into your belly.

Keep your shoulders and chest relaxed and still, while noticing your belly rising and falling with each inhalation and exhalation.

Explore the effect of the breath. What happens if you take a slightly deeper breath and then exhale while letting go of any tension in your body and face?

Pause for a comfortable few moments after exhaling. There is a silent space there, a calmness you might discover with practice, which many athletes use as a focal point for their mindful relaxation.

Pay attention to the breath and be mindful when your mind wanders, as it inevitably will, and just patiently return your attention to the breath.

Accept whatever you feel now as being what is now. Avoid judging yourself. Just focus and breathe, and when you realise your mind has drifted, bring it carefully back to the breath.

What did you experience during this activity?

Would you be able to make this a daily practice? (If so, consider using resources available from the website)

The key to Centred Breathing is to do it, without judgement. Some sessions will be more relaxing and focused than others; but the key is perseverance, because the value comes from the consistent application.

Practice Tip: There can't be such a thing as bad centring practice, because either you stay in the moment, or you spend your time bringing your thoughts back. If it's the latter, then it's much like doing repetitions in the weight room or throwdowns in the nets. Weights build body strength, and centring builds mind strength.

Important Guide Points for Centred Breathing.

Lighten your expectations

The wandering mind is perfectly natural, so a good mindful breathing session is one you do irrespective of what happens. Leave aside any self-criticism and accept what is.

Train to strengthen the core	Developing your centring skills and practices is like strengthening your "mental core". Quietening your mind and body, and gently directing your attention back into the moment, will pay big dividends. Just ten minutes a day will produce benefits.
Find the quiet space	When practising the breathing techniques, use the exhale to release tension. The space between your breaths will become the quiet centre.
Practise	All practice is valuable, and the more you observe your breath and patiently guide your attention back into the present, the more resilient these skills will be when you are in pressure situations.

A majority of my clients across sport and business have a daily practice of some form of mindfulness relaxation and meditation, which helps them stay calm and composed in high stress situations.

As Tim Gallwey, author of *The Inner Game of Tennis* (1979), noted:

....

When the mind is fastened to the rhythm of breathing, it tends to become absorbed and calm. Whether on or off the court I know of no better way to begin to deal with anxiety than to place the mind on one's breathing process.

....

MINDFUL PRACTICE 3: Quieten Your Inner Critic.

Most cricketers recognise their own inner critic telling them things like:

- *I'm never going to take wickets on this pitch*
- *I'm hopeless at playing the short ball*
- *I hope I don't drop a catch.*

The inner critic is really just trying to protect you; but it stirs up nervousness, anxiety, and worry by all-or-nothing thinking (success or disaster), rehearsing mistakes (dropping catches, being dismissed early), and focusing on weaknesses (playing the short ball, bowling in windy conditions).

Mindful Cricket cultivates composure by helping you to be more aware of how self-limiting thoughts drive feelings, and what you can do to lean into those uncomfortable feelings and take back control.

ACTIVITY: Quietening Your Inner Critic.

This mindful activity will help you to cultivate self-belief and composure by quietening your inner critic and replacing it with an inner coach. This tool is available at **www.mindfulcricket.com**.

Follow the three-step personal change process of **Awareness, Acceptance** and **Action**:

1. Awareness of how the critic limits your thinking
2. Acceptance that it's your thinking stirring up uncomfortable emotions
3. Action to coach yourself to be mindful and composed.

TOOL 1: Awareness - Meet Your Critic.

Can you recall times when you've been held back by unhelpful negative thoughts about (a) mistakes, (b) losing, or (c) worrying about other's approval?

These are the three most common ways the inner critic eats away at confidence and composure, so take a few moments to reflect on times when you've had this experience and how it made you feel and act. Use the real-life examples from a Club Cricketer in the boxes to guide you.

Mistakes: I want to avoid mistakes because they are embarrassing.

Example: *"Frustrated at training when playing poor shots, and that just made it worse. Tentative bowling in my opening over. Hoping a catch didn't come my way last week after I dropped an easy one early in the match."*

Losing: I want to avoid losing because I want to prove I am good at cricket.

Example: *"Got really annoyed when dismissed and threw the bat. Angry we lost the match and I think that was just showing that I'd lost composure. Too focused on the outcome!"*

Approval: I want to be liked because I am part of a team or club.

Example: *"Anxious so I didn't want to speak up at team meeting. I'm thinking a lot about what to do to get approval of the senior players instead of just playing my own game."*

Creating this list will help you to be aware of the connection between your thoughts, feelings and how you act.

An inner critic tends to be quite irrational or "over-the-top" in their assessment of situations. That's why I find it very helpful to guide players to create an "inner coach" and be quite deliberate in challenging their self-critical commentary.

The table below shows the contrast between "critic" and "coach":

	What an Inner Critic Believes	What an Inner Coach Believes
Mistakes	It's embarrassing making mistakes. I should avoid putting myself in that situation. Mistakes show I'm not good enough.	Mistakes are part of learning. Get comfortable with being uncomfortable. Mistakes are the pathway to getting better.
Losing	I'm only a good cricketer when I'm in form. Winning proves I'm good. It's important to be better than others.	I'm a good cricketer. Form and winning come and go. My aim is to be the best I can be.
Approval	People won't like me if I'm different. Don't try my newest delivery in matches. Follow what others are doing.	People aren't thinking about me. I have some unique strengths. Trying new things is important.

When you look at the thoughts above, it's not hard to imagine how a bit of game pressure fires up the critic and upsets composure by turning our attention towards weaknesses and difficulties. The good news is you are now mindful of how your thinking affects the way you behave, which means you can choose to do something about it if you want to.

TOOL 2: Acceptance - It's Your Critic in Action.

When the inner critic takes over, it is helpful to realise it's not the thought driving your behaviour, it's how you react to the uncomfortable feeling. For example, frustration about mistakes doesn't have to be acted on. You can choose to let the feelings roll through, because it's unlikely they'll last for more than 30-90 seconds at the most.

You can go towards the challenge despite the feelings, or you can let them control you. It's your choice.

Your Task Over the Next Two Weeks

Be observant of when your inner critic shows up. For example, you might notice you are thinking about what could go wrong before going out to bat, or at times in the field you could be hoping the ball won't come to you.

This three-step process will help reduce the power the critic has over you:

STEP 1	Pause for a moment and just notice your thoughts and the feelings they are creating. Don't judge, don't try to change them. Just accept them as they are.
STEP 2	Using your Centred Breathing skills, take between one and three breaths (depending on the situation). Be the observer of those feelings, and don't react immediately to them.
STEP 3	Choose your response. It's your choice to lean into the uncomfortable feelings and remain composed in the way you think and move.

Jot down a few thoughts on this activity when you've done it, but be mindful not to judge yourself harshly:

Practice Tip: Remember the Centred Breathing exercise, when you just observed your feelings without judging them? That's training you to let feelings rollover instead of driving you to action.

TOOL 3: Action - Give Your Inner Coach Equal Time.

As you get better at pausing to observe the inner critic (instead of immediately reacting), there is a perfect opportunity to engage your "inner coach". For example, if you beat the bat twice with perfect outswingers and then get hit for four and become really agitated with yourself and the batsman, the critic is around!

The solution just builds on the three-step process:

STEP 1: Pause and observe the critic and the effects on your feelings.

STEP 2: Breathe.

STEP 3: Ask this coaching question: *What's the basic thing to do here?*

That simple question will get you out of your own head and feelings and focused on the actions needed to move forward.

Try It Now.

Imagine you are bowling, and the inner critic is stirring up uncomfortable feelings like frustration about a dropped catch, or anxiety about not getting a wicket.

Pause and observe the critic. Breathe.

What's the basic thing to do here? (eg relax grip, focus on rhythm, use your stock ball etc)

When you use this simple approach, you might be amazed at how often you've been letting the critic run the show, and how easy it is to quieten that down and coach yourself to be more effective.

Chapter Takeaways.

A noisy mind and inner critic work against composure. However, you can build three lines of defence by accepting your uncomfortable emotions, using stillness and Centred Breathing to find calmness, and replacing that inner critic with a more rational inner coach.

Jot down your insights from this Chapter:

Quotes from the *Mindful Cricket* book :

Cultivating Composure is not the absence of emotion.

....

Centred Breathing is the core practice and gateway to composure.

....

Mindful Cricket cultivates composure by helping you to be more aware of how self-limiting thoughts drive feelings, and what you can do to take back control.

....

We all have an inner critic, and it stirs up emotions with limiting thoughts. Watch them, let the feelings roll through, and be your own inner coach: take a breath, observe, and then go back to Basics.

....

CHAPTER 7

Focus In The Moment.

3 things you'll gain from this Chapter

1. How to focus on what matters
2. Resetting concentration for each delivery
3. Drills to sharpen your focus

The Distracted Mind.

Even when we want to remain settled and focused in the present moment, our minds go to what interests them most (driven by feelings).

> *What if I get hit for another boundary? thinks the bowler walking back to their mark. I'll be taken off and not get another chance. Distracted, they amble in, serve up an inviting full toss and watch helplessly as the batsman drives hard and straight into the bowler's end stumps.*

True concentration cannot be forced, yet coaches instruct players to concentrate harder without giving them any advice about helpful ways to actually do it. Telling someone to concentrate is like telling someone to score runs. Great idea - but how?

Practice Tip: Your mind will NOT stay in the present moment - it will wander. Mindful Cricket is about developing the ability to bring your mind back onto what matters, when it matters.

Self-Assessment

Would you like to see the ball earlier, bowl with subtle variation, and reset your focus time and again across the longest of batting or bowling innings? If the answer is *yes,* then complete the assessment below to identify your strengths and potential areas for improvement.

Instructions:
Reflect on the statements below, one at a time, and use the five-point scale to consider to what extent you agree or disagree.

1 Strongly Disagree **2** Disagree **3** Neither Agree Nor Disagree **4** Agree **5** Strongly Agree

	Batting	Bowling	Fielding/Keeping
Ball Focus	I really focus on the ball and take it one delivery at a time.	I plan and execute my bowling plans one ball at a time.	I am fully focused and positive as the bowler delivers the ball.
Feel Focus	I have a comfortable stance, and good feel and timing for shots.	I can make changes in my rhythm and hand to create subtle variation.	I move with rhythm and catch with soft hands.
Focus Reset	I can reset my focus after playing a poor shot or losing concentration.	I can set aside distracting thoughts and refocus on my bowling rhythm.	I switch my focus on when needed.

The statements which you have rated 3, 2 or 1 are potential areas for development.

Priorities for Development.

Which areas of improvement will have the greatest positive impact on your cricket?

The art of the great batsman is to see the ball earlier. The art of the great bowler is subtle variation. The art of the wicket-keeper is to set and reset their concentration ball by ball, hour on hour. They don't concentrate harder - they focus all their senses on their craft in the moment.

The keys to concentration are remarkably simple:
- Really watch the ball with curiosity *(Ball Focus)*
- Master rhythm, feel and touch **(Touch and Feel)**
- Switch focus on and off as needed **(Resetting)**.

Let's explore some of the core activities and drills from the *Mindful Cricket* book and courses, to lay a foundation for your concentration.

MINDFUL PRACTICE 1: Watch the Ball with Curiosity.

Cricketers and coaches have talked about watching the ball since the game began, yet do you really know how to watch the ball? Do you practise watching the ball, or is your attention on technique and scoring runs while the ball just happens to be a part of the process?

The following activities include net drills together with brief accounts from players of their experience with this approach. As mentioned earlier, many of these are inspired by the work of Tim Gallwey.

BATTING ACTIVITY: Discover the Detail of the Ball.

This activity brings you back to the most basic of cricket skills - watching the ball. It is intended to build awareness of what that actually means.

Instructions:
- Find a cricket ball and open your mind to seeing and doing things that might at first seem too simple and obvious. Persevere.
- Place it where you can observe it from many angles, but don't touch it. Take a few Centred Breaths to calm your mind, then set your attitude to be as curious as a child seeing a cricket ball for the first time. Avoid judging the activity, just do it for 3-5 minutes.
- What do you see?
- What colour is the ball? What changes in shading do you observe across its parts?
- What is that thing around the middle of the ball? A seam? Can you observe more than five things about the seam? Colour, material, consistency, thickness, threading...?
- How is the surface of the ball? Rough, smooth, shiny? Is it four pieces or two?
- Is it round? Any dents or imperfections? Anything else you can see?

When you've studied the ball, sit back, take three Centred Breaths and consider the Reflection Questions about how you watch the ball when batting.

Do you really seek out the ball and lock onto it like a sharp spotlight?

Do you see the seam and study its spin or swing?

Do you watch it with relaxed concentration, or are you more strained and tense?

Do you sense the possibility of improvement from going back to the most basic instruction in cricket – "watch the ball"?

BATTING ACTIVITY: Spot the Seam.

This activity taps into your natural skills of concentration and focus as you look for the seam of the ball. With practice it can help you to relax and see the ball and its pathway more easily.

Instructions:

- To practise your ball focus, allocate 5-10 minutes in a batting net with a medium-pace bowler or someone doing throwdowns. (No bouncers, to make sure you are safe and focused.)
- Take your stance, use your usual forward or back press, and instead of just watching the ball or thinking about your shot, put all your attention on how early and sharply you can see the seam of the ball after it's delivered.
- Don't be concerned about playing good shots or being dismissed. Clear your mind, be composed, and see if you can trust your natural instincts to play the shot. Just aim to bring "active calmness".
- It might feel strange to be so relaxed, or to be looking for a part of the ball. Initially you might feel you won't be ready; however, your mind is like a well-functioning computer, so if you feed it the right information, it will make the right decision.
- And your coach is always there to help with the technique when it's needed.

Here is an example, recorded in a Player's Journal, of how this simple drill changed their focus:

PLAYER'S JOURNAL

Eddie (Club Cricketer): *I tried the curious mind approach to batting and it was amazing what happened. For the first five minutes of every practice session I really focused on looking for the seam. It took a few sessions to do it and be calm and alert, but I soon realised how badly I'd been focusing before, so I just made it my normal practice. I then added the thought to let the ball come to me, which meant I was playing as late as possible. Pretty soon I was picking up the line and swing really early. It's helped me to be much more relaxed and balanced early in my innings, and I'm letting balls go when I would normally have poked at them.*

MINDFUL PRACTICE 2: Master Touch, Feel and Rhythm.

Think for a moment about what cricketers take for granted: how a bowler adjusts their point of release by millimetres to change the length of delivery by half a metre or a batsman deftly dabs a late cut. These are the skills of craftsmen, and they make you realise it is close to a miracle of coordination when you just toss the ball accurately back to the bowler!

The *Mindful Cricket* book and programs feature a range of drills for batsmen, bowlers, field and keepers to help build concentration skills. Here are three brief examples to get started:

DRILL 1: Eyes Closed Bowling

Pick up a ball and find the side of a net where you can bowl the ball safely without any risk to you or others. Close your eyes and bowl the ball into the net off one step.

Repeat this a few times, being particularly mindful of observing where and how you feel the rhythm in your delivery.

What do you notice?
Which parts of your body are involved?
What triggers the movement?
Which muscles flow together?
What's different between deliveries that have rhythm and those that don't?

This type of eyes-closed exercise is regularly practised by Olympic archers who will think nothing of spending half an hour in eyes-closed practice to get in touch with the feeling of releasing the arrow. Basketballers do the same for free throws. Why don't bowlers do it more often in cricket?

DRILL 2: Batting Sound and Feel

Pick up a bat and ask someone to do a few throwdowns in the net.

Instead of thinking of technique or shots, focus only on the sound and feel of the ball hitting the bat. You'll know when it's in the sweet spot.

Most players find it best to do this drill with throwdowns, but pretty soon they're ready to take it into full-scale net practice. I've had many players say it's a great way to break out of bad form patches.

What do you notice?
Is there a special sound when the ball hits the middle?
How does focusing on the sound shift your focus?
Do you find yourself less bothered about technique and more trusting of your instincts?

This incredibly simple drill can have a huge effect on batting focus and confidence, by taking the mind off technical details and tapping into natural rhythm and timing. Use it when you are struggling with form.

DRILL 3: Hold Your Bowling Shape

This drill is one of a series in Mindful Cricket designed to challenge bowlers to retain their shape when faced with challenges from the game.

Mark out your usual run-up and have a teammate stand about 2-3 metres from the bowler's stumps. Agree a set of six target areas: three outside off (short, length and full), and three at middle and off. Number them from 1-6.

As you pass your teammates and approach the stumps, they tell you a number to hit the required length or line.

Your practice challenge is to deliver the ball with rhythm and energy to the target they've just given you. It's fun and a very good test of whether you can keep your body cues consistent, which means holding your shape.

What do you notice?	What thoughts help or hinder your ability to hold your shape? Are there cues that are basic to staying in shape? What other drills can you use the strengthen your focus on holding shape?

PLAYER'S JOURNAL INSIGHTS

Hershelle (Club Cricketer – Off-Spinner): *I never really thought that focusing on my rhythm was important for concentration, but it's been really good. At every practice session I do some drills with the other spinners to reinforce our cues and shape for rhythm. We can see what each other is doing and we can help out. For example, my best action is when I rotate high over the top, and my teammates remind me in games and I'm definitely bowling more accurately and with more bounce.*

MINDFUL PRACTICE 3: Reset Your Focus.

Cricket, like archery, baseball and golf, is a "stop-start" sport, meaning that players focus intensely for short periods, then drop the intensity, and then focus again.

It's essential to learn and practise switching concentration on and off, so it doesn't fade when needed most. That's why resetting is one of the key practices to strengthening your Game Mindset skills.

ACTIVITY: 1-2-3 Reset Your Concentration.

Whether you are batting, bowling, fielding or keeping, there's a simple ritual you can use to switch on concentration. It is about owning your space. It builds perfectly from the work on breathing, ball focus and touch and feel.

A video of the 1-2-3 Reset method is available at **www.mindfulcricket.com**.

STEP 1	Look down and step slightly away. Take a slow, deep breath, exhale firmly while rolling your shoulders and loosening your arms. Pause for just a moment.
STEP 2	Grip the bat, taking care like a golfer to place it comfortably and securely in both hands. Let your gaze shift from hands to the horizon as you think about readying for the next delivery.
STEP 3	Move at your pace into your stance, tap the bat twice, and quietly but firmly say under your breath: "Where's the ball?" as you watch the bowler approach.

WHERE AND WHEN WILL YOU USE 1-2-3 RESET?

One of the most obvious examples of the use of reset in sport is the professional tennis player. Watch a game and you'll see player after player use 1-2-3 Reset: breathing and loosening, flicking the strings of their racquet, and then moving into their serve or receiving position.

I observed Cheteshwar Pujara use a similar approach to reset his mind, ball after ball, when his three centuries in four Tests helped India win their first series in Australia.

Where and when will you use 1-2-3 Reset? (eg at the start of an innings, for each delivery when batting or bowling, fielding in slips, and after a dropped catch)

What call to action will you use? (eg off-spin bowlers use cues like "Up and Over" to remind themselves to get energy and height into the delivery)

Chapter Takeaways.

The art of the great batsman is to see the ball earlier. The art of the great bowler is subtle variation. The art of the wicket-keeper is to set and reset their concentration ball by ball, hour on hour. All are about focusing in the moment, and having the skills to bring a wandering mind back to what matters.

Jot down your insights from this Chapter:

Quotes from the *Mindful Cricket* book:

You already have the ability to focus in the moment. It's a natural part of the Blue Zone, so it's not a question of finding a new Game Mindset, but tapping into what you already have.

....

Curiosity sits at the heart of concentration, and in cricket there are three things to get really curious about: the ball; mastering rhythm, timing and touch; and resetting focus when it's needed.

....

Make 1-2-3 Reset a ritual you can rely on in any situation.

....

Cricketers and coaches have talked about watching the ball since the game began, but do you really know how to watch the ball? Do you practise watching the ball, or is your attention on technique and scoring runs?

....

CHAPTER 8

Keep It Simple.

3 things you'll gain from this Chapter

1. Understand why Keeping It Simple matters
2. How to create a simple "Go-To-Plan"
3. Confidence in your game Basics

Overthinking.

It's difficult to keep things simple, particularly in the moments that matter. With the best of intentions, we overthink by trying to control all that's happening. Add to that the advice from well-meaning teammates or observers, and things become so complicated we forget the Basics that matter!

Imagine that a team needs eight runs to win at the start of the last over of a 20/20 final. The mindful player is composed, weighs up the best scoring options and then settles with relaxed aggression, waiting on the bowler. With timing and placement, they easily pick off the runs in twos.

What a contrast to the player who, thinking they must hit a boundary, swings hard at the first ball, lifts their eyes too early, and drags the ball waist-high to mid-wicket, leaving a new batsman with an even tougher challenge.

The Power of Simplicity.

The *Mindful Cricket* book features the story of an English County player who had success in the T20 Leagues but was struggling with his game. His Journal highlights what happens to a player's mind when things get too complicated:

My mind is jumbled and racing out on the ground. I'm thinking about so many things it's impossible to be calm and focused. I'm worrying about bowling to batsmen with big powerful bats on tiny grounds. The noisy crowds and comments from the opposition are bothering me more than normal. I'm also feeling the pressure of a one-year contract. Instead of bowling four tight overs, I'm reacting too much, and the past two innings I've had to go for it from the first ball and holed out both times with pretty ordinary shots.

The Secret to Simplicity - Go-To-Plans.

One of the best ways to develop a mindset of simplicity is to create Go-To-Plans, which is a simple tool built on three Mindful Practices:

1. Back to Basics
2. Play to Your Strengths
3. Apply Pressure to opponents.

Go-To-Plans take your mind off things you can't control (like pitch conditions), and instead focus in the moment on what you can do something about.

Commitment to Basics and playing to your strengths makes it simpler, which increases the chances of success by playing the percentages; while the focus on Applying Pressure gets you out of your own head.

Let's develop plans for batting and bowling practice, so you can understand the foundation thinking and action behind this very valuable tool. You'll then be ready to take the approach into matches.

ACTIVITY 1: Create a "Library" for Your Go-To-Plan.

You can use Go-To-Plans in lots of different situations (eg start of innings, when struggling, final overs of a match, etc). It's useful to have thought through some options, because in those moments the plan needs to be super simple.

TOOL 1: Back to Basics.

Consider the Basics to fall back on when batting, bowling and fielding/keeping.

Draft a "library list" of important Basics for your game in each activity:

Bowling	Batting	Fielding/Keeping
Example: *Stick to line and length*	Example: *Use 1-2-3 Reset*	Example: *Watch ball into hands*

Add to your Go-To-Plan library as you complete other Mindful Cricket activities.

TOOL 2: Play to Your Strengths.

The second part of a Go-To-Plan is to capitalise on strengths, because in any match situation the ideal thing to do is to leverage your strengths.

Here's an example of a My Strengths Toolsheet for batting and bowling for the County Player:

My Strengths Toolsheet	
What I Bring to Bowling	**What I Bring to Batting**
Spin both ways	Sound defence
Can read a batsman	Enough power to hit over the ring
Accurate	Range of shots
Experience and success in different conditions	Experience and success in different conditions
Subtle variation of pace	Quick between wickets

When the mind gets complicated, it is easy to lose sight of strengths and become overwhelmed by the challenges and weaknesses. That's why being mindful is so helpful - a couple of breaths, a reminder of strengths, and soon things look so much better.

Create your own My Strengths list (get assistance from your coaches):

My Strengths Toolsheet

Bowling	Batting	Fielding/Keeping
Example: *Subtle variations*	Example: *Good defence*	Example: *Taking sharp catches*

TOOL 3: Apply Pressure.

The third foundation in a Go-To-Plan is Applying Pressure to opponents. This has the double benefit of getting you out of your own head, and also doing things which can shift momentum.

The whole Section on Play Clever will provide ideas and practical content; however, take a few moments now to reflect on some of the ways you can apply pressure to opponents.

List ideas on how to Apply Pressure to your opponents:

Apply Pressure Toolsheet

Bowling	Batting	Fielding/Keeping
Example: *Restrict scoring*	Example: *Quick singles*	Example: *Cut off boundaries*

Practice Tip: The power of a Go-To-Plan lies less in the content of the plan, and more in the confidence and focus that come from having one to fall back on when things are tight.

With your library taking shape, a good next step is to create Go-To-Plans for batting and bowling practice to get familiar with this approach.

ACTIVITY 2: Creating a Batting Practice Go-To-Plan.

A Go-To-Plan should be brief, and built on three components: Back to Basics, Play to Your Strengths, and Apply Pressure to opponents. Keep It Simple and build your focus and confidence, so less is better. I recommend putting it onto a card so you have a quick reference point during the practice session.

Also give thought before batting practice to a "game scenario" you might work on, such as starting an innings, or chasing down a score. This will help to simulate the thought processes.

Go-To-Plan for Batting Practice

What Basics are important? *(eg early into position, short backlift, head still and watch the ball)*

What strengths can you bring? *(eg solid defence, quick to judge length)*

How do you Apply Pressure to bowlers? *(eg start with positive body language, clip anything on leg)*

ACTIVITY 3: Creating a Bowling Practice Go-To-Plan.

Create your bowling plan using the same process as for batting. For example, you might want to work on your "death" bowling in a short form game.

Go-To-Plan for Bowling Practice

What Basics are important? *(eg bowl to one part of the field, maintain rhythm)*

What strengths can you bring? *(eg slower ball, accuracy)*

How do you Apply Pressure? *(eg first two deliveries yorkers outside off, follow a blocked run with slower ball because batter is likely frustrated)*

Practice Tip: Use exactly the same approach for developing and using Go-To-Plans in matches. With experience you'll be able to create these on the run, by drawing from your "library" and match awareness.

Chapter Takeaways.

Mindful Cricketers don't try to control everything. They do take time to set and hone their Go-To-Plans, which means that when it's not working or confidence starts to waver, there is something tried and tested to fall back on.

Jot down your insights from this Chapter:

Quotes from the *Mindful Cricket* book:

"Simple" begins with a mindset of focusing on the Basics, Playing to Your Strengths and Applying Pressure.

....

Mindful Cricket is attending to what you can control, and guiding your mind away from the uncontrollable.

....

Apply Pressure to your opponents through projecting confidence in your body language, and using your strengths and the Basics.

....

The Go-To-Plan is a simple approach seen in the mindset and behaviours of cricketers who own their space and hold their shape when others are losing theirs.

....

CHAPTER 9

Adapt Fast.

3 things you'll gain from this Chapter

1. Learn how to adapt fast
2. Bring a new mindset to practising your game
3. How to Plan-Do-Check-Adapt

Players Need to Adapt - Cricket Practice Hasn't.

Cricket requires players to adapt or adjust to change. The ball, the pitch, weather, players and the game itself all bring difference, and we need to learn and adapt so success isn't restricted to when conditions are favourable.

Observe a top batsman when they're not picking the spin. Can you see them adjusting their game, searching for ways to survive and get on top? Every ball is a mini experiment: batting on off stump to take LBW out of the picture or using their feet to get to pitch of the ball, maybe getting back or coming down the pitch to hit the bowler off their length or sweeping anything on the stumps.

These examples, and thousands of others, highlight how cricket is a game of adapting, of constantly thinking on your feet. Yet have you ever been trained in how to learn and adapt quickly? How can cricketers be expected to adapt fast when the traditional cricket net practice is so different to the real demands of a match? It raises a challenging question:

....

Does traditional cricket practice really help to speed up adaptability, or does it have the opposite effect of slowing down the learning process?

....

A Different Mindset.

Are you open to a more agile and adaptive approach to practising cricket, which puts responsibility on you and your teammates to lead your own practice sessions?

Instead of coach-run sessions and a meandering series of activities for batters, bowlers and fielders, practice sessions will be divided into short segments (sprints) where you work in small groups to Plan, Do, Check and Adapt fast. Coaches play a role in feedback and support, while you own the practice session and the outcomes you produce.

This approach challenges many traditional cricket ideas, but it's based on team performance methods used across the business world, and increasingly in sporting teams who want to be more adaptive.

Reflection Questions

How well does current net practice really prepare you for match situations?

What are the obvious differences between nets and matches?

Do you create game scenarios at practice to simulate match challenges?

Are you open to a more dynamic approach where you Plan, Do, Check and Adapt in small teams?

Plan–Do–Check-Adapt (PDCA).

Consider the batsman and the hard-to-pick spinner. The batsman is constantly planning, doing, checking what's working and then adapting. Can you see the "learning loop" that's happening in the batsman's mind?

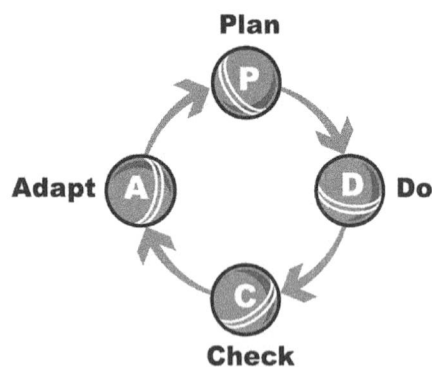

P: Create the Plan
D: Do it
C: Check what worked and was learned
A: Adapt

Then PDCA again, and again and again, with a Clear Mind and a nice balance of Play Brave and Play Clever. One ball at a time, simple and effective. That's thinking on your feet and playing Mindful Cricket.

Operating Rhythm.

PDCA (Plan-Do-Check-Adapt) is a derivation of the continuous improvement method popularised by Edwards Deming, an American engineer and pioneer of the Quality Management field.

Here's how I apply it to a net session *(see* **www.mindfulcricket.com** *for more details)*:

Example of a PDCA Net Session	
Players are allocated into small teams, with each team responsible for their own training and development. Each team has mini-whiteboards or equivalent, so each player can quickly jot down plans and scores. This visual display is important.	
Plan	The players choose the overall goals for the session; what they want to work on (skills, game scenarios, etc); and the operating rhythm, ie when they pause to check in on what's been achieved and learned. Usually in a net of three bowlers the rhythm is 18 deliveries per set (called a "sprint").
Do	In a set of 18 deliveries, each player works on one specific skill or scenario (eg a technical skill, or simulating a game situation such as the opening three overs of a game). The players or coaches measure how successful they are and everybody offers feedback to each other.
Check	At the end of each sprint (18 deliveries), the team pauses to reflect on what's been achieved, the learning, any blocks or barriers, and what they will do in the next set. They can change the sprint length if it's too short or too long.
Adapt	Players take learnings into the next sets and into future sessions. A typical practice will have a series of sprints with the PDCA loop. The intention is always to have good quality over quantity, and fast learning.
Do you see opportunities to make your net sessions more interesting and challenging by bringing a PDCA mindset and approach?	

ACTIVITY: Transform Your Personal Net Practice (PDCA).

This activity will help you to get familiar with PDCA thinking by using it as a personal process to get the most from a net session.

Instructions:

Choose a net session and use that to begin applying PDCA. Think of it in three segments – batting, bowling and fielding. In each segment you will use the PDCA to practise mindfully.

Plan

Prior to each session, decide on two specific skills or practices for each segment to work on during that session. For example, in fielding you migt choose a quick pick-up throw and taking high running catches. Decide your goal for each and write it down.

Do

Divide up your batting, bowling and fielding time so that you focus on one skill or practice at a time.

Batting	Bowling	Fielding

Check

Pause once during each segment, and again at the end of each segment, to get feedback from your coach or teammates and to reflect on three questions:

What has worked?

What have I learned?

What needs further improvement?

Batting	Bowling	Fielding

Adapt

At the end of practice, review what worked, where improvement is needed, and how you will act on those ideas.

Reflection Questions

What effect did the PDCA loop have on your focus and quality of practice?

What worked well that you'd continue doing?

What improvements could you make?

Are you interested in using PDCA to build better learning loops in your day-to-day life?

Taking PDCA Mindset to the Next Level.

The key to adaptive thinking is the mindset of learning by doing. That means thinking on your feet in shorter time frames, using the PDCA process to test and learn.

In the *Mindful Cricket* book there are more detailed instructions on how to use PDCA as a way of planning and navigating your life on a week-to-week basis.

Here is a journal entry from a State level player who started with the PDCA process. His account provides a really nice example of how adaptive thinking is about learning and refining as you move forward:

PLAYER'S JOURNAL

When I started with PDCA, I wondered if the post-it notes and daily stand-up process was a bit over the top, and I didn't really expect a lot of value, but agreed to give it a four-week test.

In the first week, if I was 100% honest, I pretty much just went through the motions. However, it was the review at the end of the first sprint that started the change.

I'd achieved very little in that first week, so I started to get a lot more specific about my daily tasks, and the momentum built from there. By week three I was putting more projects into the plan because the PDCA was just so good at getting me efficient and nimble in making improvements and getting things done.

My Performance Coach suggested we bring PDCA into the net practice, and we applied it in three ways which all had value.

This mindset and approach have the potential to transform the way cricketers plan, prepare for and play cricket. We've barely scratched the surface here, but there will be many more resources available on **www.mindfulcricket.com** as the Mindful Cricket community adopts this approach and shares experiences.

Chapter Takeaways.

Cricket is constantly changing. No two pitches are the same, all bowlers are different, and even balls that look the same behave differently. The game changes in an instant with a dropped catch, two quick wickets or even lucky edges through slips.

You can't play cricket successfully without the ability to adapt to the conditions and the game itself. It is a conservative game with many traditions and myths that restrict and even work against players and coaches learning and adapting fast. Without the mindset and skills to quickly learn and adapt, batsmen misjudge the pace of the pitch, keepers let through countless byes, and bowlers serve deliveries right into batsmen's strengths. That's no way to play a game that is constantly changing.

Jot down your insights from this Chapter:

Quotes from the *Mindful Cricket* book:

Cricket is a game of constantly thinking on your feet and adapting quickly. The ball, the pitch, weather, players and the game itself all bring difference.

....

Mindful Cricket is learning and adapting so success isn't restricted to when conditions are favourable.

....

The PDCA Learning Loop is thinking and planning on your feet, and it's learning by doing. It is embedding action debriefing to capture the lessons learned, highlighting and celebrating success, avoiding the repeating of mistakes, and moving on from setbacks.

....

Use PDCA to get more from net sessions, to be more effective in planning your week, and in building the habit of thinking on your feet.

....

Pillar 2.
Play Brave

PILLAR 2: Play Brave.

Have you read the speech by US President Theodore Roosevelt (1910) featuring this powerful quote?

....

The credit belongs to the man who is actually in the arena, whose face is marred by dust and sweat and blood; who strives valiantly; who errs, who comes short again and again...who at the best knows in the end the triumph of high achievement, and who at the worst, if he fails, at least fails while daring greatly.

....

When the ball is flying around your ears, when the physical training is tough, and when you have difficult life decisions to make, there's a place for a bravery and a spirit of character which Roosevelt's words capture brilliantly.

If you are brave, you are feeling fear. Isn't bravery the absence of fear? No, because fear is what you feel when exposed and vulnerable and don't know what's going to happen. Bravery is facing down and going forward despite your fears, which are so often driven by the "villains" of self-doubt, fear of failure and giving up.

Mindful Cricket confronts those villains which chip away at confidence and composure, by challenging you to set a Bold Vision, to Put It On the Line and Hold the Tension long enough to reap the rewards.

CHAPTER 10

Create Your Bold Vision.

3 things you'll gain from this Chapter

1. A Bold Vision to inspire and guide you
2. Performance Road Map for the next 90 days
3. Confidence in your direction and priorities

Bold Mindset.

Players who play to win do better than those who play to avoid losing. However, sometimes instead of daring to be great, we aim too low and fall short of our potential.

The case for "daring greatly" is compelling, but what can you do to tap the inner reserve of strength to win the tug-of-war between self-doubt and desire for success? You start with being bold and clear about who you are and what you want to achieve in cricket and beyond, and then refine that into a 90-day Performance Road Map.

Go for What You Want.

Everyone knows goals are important, but few things lift and sustain performance more than the combination of a Bold Vision and clear performance goals.

Bold Vision.

This is looking beyond the short-term time horizon and asking yourself: *What do I want?*, rather than drifting towards the future or asking more tentative questions such as: *What do I think is possible?*

Performance Goals.

These are the shorter-term targets to aim towards. They are stepping stones towards your Bold Vision, and provide a sense of focus and confidence.

Bold Vision	Do you have a vision or dream of the future that really motivates you to put in time and effort to improve your game, or do you tend to take it as it comes?
Stretch	Is your vision bold and beyond what is currently possible, or is it more "low bar" with few risks or stretch?
Clarity	Do you regularly set and write down clear, challenging but attainable short-term to medium-term goals for your cricket, or are they vague and unrealistic?
Consistency	Do you consistently use your goals to help navigate through setbacks and challenges, or do you tend to get caught up in micro-details, like obstacles and low-quality practice?

MINDFUL PRACTICE 1: Find Your True North.

A clear and bold vision gives you the clarity of direction to make plans and decisions. It is like the "True North" for a yachtsman who, despite constant changes in direction to avoid danger and to capitalise on favourable winds, always knows their core intention is to head for True North.

I recommend you do the True North activity for all areas of your life (eg study, career, etc). The instructions are based on that approach, but if you prefer to just focus on cricket, then do so.

ACTIVITY: Create Your Personal True North.

For this activity you will need a pen and ideally a pack of post-it notes (or sheets of paper cut into approximately 30-40 post-it note sized pieces). Putting your thinking onto these small pieces will help you to be more flexible in developing and sorting ideas and priorities. You can use the space below as an alternative, but the smaller pieces of paper will help you to sort through and prioritise the many different options.

STEP 1: Identify the Most Important Areas of Your Life.

What are the most important areas of your life? For example, a Cricket Academy Player doing this exercise chose five areas: *Cricket, Fitness, Study, Social* and *Family*.

Write down each Important Area on a separate post-it, and draw a border around it so you can see these are different from the notes you will be creating in the next steps.

Examples of Areas:

Cricket	Fitness	Study	Social	Family

Notes:

STEP 2: Prioritise the Areas.

Sort the Important Areas notes into priority order to truly reflect what is most important to you. Be sure to choose the order which reflects your real priorities, and not what others want you to do.

Prioritisation means letting go of some things in order to focus on others. This practice of letting go is a principle of mindfulness, and there are real benefits in building the habit of letting go of things that aren't so important.

Example of Priority Order:

1 Cricket	**2** Fitness	**3** Study	**4** Social	**5** Family

Notes:

STEP 3: Think Bold - Define What You Want to Achieve.

On the remaining post-it notes, jot down all the things you want to achieve in each of the Important Areas.

What time horizon would you like to use for this activity? As a guide, many people and teams use two Horizons: H#1 is short-term (12 months) and H#2 is mid-term to longer-term (1-3 years).

Be bold and creative. Jot one item per note to generate a spread of post-it notes with anything that comes to mind. If you struggle to think of ideas, just ask yourself the question: What will success look like?

Example of items in each area:

1. Cricket	2. Fitness	3. Study	4. Social	5. Family
Average 40 plus next season	Be in top 20% of squad	Nail my final year exams	Keep balance right	Make Mum and Dad proud
Get a 20/20 contract	Awesome flexibility	Get into Uni Commerce Degree Course	Keep a solid relationship with partner	Support my little brother

Play an International	No injuries	Graduate in Commerce	Maintain friends from school	Make time each quarter for family event
Build a business career in sport	No limitations from fitness	Get career in Sports Management	Build new network	Be a positive influence

STEP 4: Find the True North Items.

When you've created what feels like a full list across the key areas, step back and ask yourself:

....

Are there one or two Horizon #2 ambitions that are the most compelling "big picture" items?

....

These are likely to be your True North.

Example of the Cricket Academy Player's True North and Journal Report:

1. Get into University Commerce Course and graduate to set me up to work in a business career connected to sport
2. Secure a contract for one 20/20 League.

PLAYER'S JOURNAL

My True North exercise was a bit of mess to start with, but the post-it notes really helped to get my thinking clear. It took me about a month to really land the two True North items, but since then it's been amazing in getting me organised.

The first True North is to get into University and graduate with a Commerce Degree, which sets me up to work in sport as a business. That's more than three years away, but it's definitely a Bold Vision. The second True North is to get a contract in one of the 20/20 Leagues. Writing down that vision has been really valuable in getting me focused.

Write up Your Draft True North.

Take a few minutes to summarise the key items in your True North, so you can align your longer-term vision and 12-month goals. This may take some time to fully refine, but you have the starting point.

My True North

The next activity will bring your big vision into a 90-day Performance Road Map.

MINDFUL PRACTICE 2:
Create Your 90-Day Performance Road Map.

How can you sustain energy and results over the "long game" which is needed to achieve a Bold Vision? Why do many sportspeople do well for short periods of time and then drop back, or even burn out?

The secret lies in understanding that sustainable performance is about:
- Achieving meaningful results
- Developing and growing
- Enjoying what you are doing
- Partnering with important other people.

The absence of even one of these four elements will make it harder to keep being at your best.

What happens when you aren't achieving meaningful results?

What happens when you aren't developing and growing?

How does your mindset and physical state change when you aren't enjoying your sport or other activities?

Why are partnering relationships with teammates, coaches and other important people so valuable?

Choosing the Right Horizon.

The acronym **ADEP** stands for **A**chievement–**D**evelopment–**E**njoyment–**P**artnering. These four elements are an excellent framework for goal setting because they are the most important ingredients for sustainable high performance. When combined with the right horizon goals and the associated actions, they will increase your chances of success.

My standard recommendation is to do this with a 90-day horizon because that is enough time to make significant progress. If that seems too far away, just bring it in to 60 or 30 days. Use PDCA thinking to test what works best for you.

ACTIVITY: Creating Your 90-Day Performance Road Map (ADEP).

Review the major items in your True North and use the template below or the Performance Road Map ADEP Toolsheet from **www.mindfulcricket.com.**

ACHIEVE

> **What are the most important goals to achieve in the next 90 days so you are headed towards your True North?**
>
> Example: *Achieve a batting average over 40 to get selected in the A-grade team next season*

DEVELOP

> **What new or improved skills, fitness and mental capabilities will you need to develop, to achieve your goals?**
>
> Example: *Complete a 6-week Mindfulness Training Course to boost composure*

ENJOY

> **What's important to make the next 90 days enjoyable and energy-giving?**
>
> Example: *Build in recovery sessions twice a week*

PARTNER

> **How can you build and sustain strong partnering relationships?**
>
> Example: *Get better alignment with coach on development priorities and plans*

Completing Your Performance Road Map.

Your Performance Road Map is a simple and powerful way to align your True North with shorter-term priorities. Refine it into a one-page plan, and then use the Seven-Point Goal Setting tool below to get clear on the actions needed to make this a reality.

TOOL: Seven- Point Goal Setting.

The seven steps are outlined below, together with a simple example for each. The full-sized template can be downloaded from **www.mindfulcricket.com**. When using this tool, make it a ritual to pause for a few moments to breathe and bring your focus calmly into the moment. It's good practice!

STEP 1   **Write down the goal**

Example: *Average at least three wickets per game*

STEP 2   **Give it a time frame**

Example: *The whole season*

STEP 3   **Confirm why it is important**

Example: *Need this level of performance and consistency to get selected in the State Team*

STEP 4   **Identify potential blocks or barriers to achieving the goal**

Example: *Flat pitches, loss of form or inconsistency*

STEP 5   **Current position in relation to goal**

Example: *Last season average was 2.5 wickets per game but inconsistent*

STEP 6   **Construct a plan with key activities**

Example: *Technique - boost accuracy across spells, and develop variations for flatter wickets*

STEP 7	**Identify key resources to achieve goal**
	Examples: *Work with coaches and trainers on fitness, technique and mindset; use Mindful Cricket Journal to track progress; use weekly sprint goals and then debrief with coaches*

Chapter Takeaways.

Players who play to win do better than those who play to avoid losing. This mindset starts with the intention to go for what you want rather than limiting yourself to what you currently see as possible. Create a Bold Vision for your future and then draft the Road Map to get there by using the ADEP elements – Achieve, Develop, Enjoy and Partner.

Jot down your insights from this Chapter:

Quotes from the *Mindful Cricket* book:

The case for daring is strong. However, that means letting go of the self-doubt that causes us to play small and expect the worst.

....

Bold Vision is a way of thinking that is proven to lead to greater success.

....

Creating a True North provides a strong sense of direction, and helps with defining shorter goals and priorities.

....

Sustained performance comes from Achieving, Developing, Enjoying and Partnering (ADEP).

....

The ADEP 90-Day Road Map is a performance framework which helps to make the True North a reality by creating a clear plan which shows priorities and actions.

....

CHAPTER 11

Put It On The Line.

3 things you'll gain from this Chapter

1. How to play with positive intent
2. Why Brilliant Basics is a winner
3. Tools to defeat perfectionism

Fear of Failure.

Some cricketers take on the game while others play to avoid mistakes. It's all a question of whether you Put It On the Line or play tentatively.

Why be tentative when we'd rather be bold? A primary reason is fear of failure, and particularly fear of being seen to fail or let others down. Tell-tale signs of fear of failure include being overly anxious, too cautious, doing better in practice than in games, or even taking reckless risks when pressure builds.

Three practices have helped many players to take on their fear of failure:

Seek success over avoiding failure	Embrace the "squirm" that comes with the possibility of failing
Do the Brilliant Basics	Build confidence and composure for the moments that matter
Defeat perfectionism and comparison	Get rid of unhelpful thoughts and motivations.

Are you more likely to be bold or tentative in a big moment?

Does fear of failure affect your cricket?

How reliable are your performances in the moments that matter?

How do you treat yourself when you make a mistake?

MINDFUL PRACTICE 1: Seek Success Over Avoiding Failure.

To do well in moments that matter requires a mindset of using the challenge to test yourself rather than being fixated on winning or losing.

That's a mindset to be vulnerable, and it says:

I know I'm going to fail. It's inevitable but it doesn't worry me. I'm in here to see how far I can push it and how good I can be.

Mindful Cricket is accepting you are vulnerable in competition. Not only can you fail, you will fail. It will sting at times, but that's part of the game, and you're strong enough to dust yourself off and get back up again.

How do we build this vulnerability? How do we make what many see as a weakness into a foundation for success? The answer is Game Mindset, and here are two activities to further build on the work you've already done to Cultivate Composure, Focus in the Moment and Create a Bold Vision.

ACTIVITY 1: Play With Intent.

Imagine you are watching two batsmen in a tight match where loss of a wicket might lose the game, but without scoring boundaries they'll fall short of the target.

Jot down differences you might see if one player brought the "Seek Success" mindset and the other the "Avoid Failure" mindset.

Seek Success

Example: *Pressuring the field with quick running*

Avoid Failure

Example: *Losing their shape and overhitting*

One thing you might notice is the difference in the intent of batsmen. For example, the batsman seeking success will own their space, and be purposeful even in their defensive shots. The player avoiding failure is more likely reacting to the intent of their opponents.

Be Mindful of Your Intent.

This mindfulness activity asks you to observe what's going on between your thoughts, feelings, and what's actually happening. By building this awareness, and using your Centred Breathing skills to hold those uncomfortable emotions, you can reduce the power of unhelpful thoughts and feelings.

Instructions:
When facing challenging situations, try this activity and then jot down your reflections on one of those situations.

Notice	**Be mindful of your intent in moments that matter.** *For example, you might notice you are more tentative in practice or match situations (eg holding back from playing shots, or trying to bowl carefully).*
	What did you notice in the situation you are reflecting on?
Observe	**Observe the feelings or emotions associated with each situation. Don't try to change the feeling; just be aware that the feeling is likely driving you to act in a certain way, such as to be more tentative or overly aggressive.**
	What feelings were involved and how did they drive your behaviour in your chosen situation?

Consider	Reflect on the mindset you bring to each situation. Consider whether it is to Put It On the Line, or to hold back.
	What was your mindset and how did that intent affect your play?
Choose	Make a conscious choice to play with intent by acting positively in ways that go towards success, rather than away from failure. (Use the Go-To-Plan Tool to help you prepare for these situations).
	In your chosen situation, what choices did you make and how did that change your feelings and actions?

This style of activity can seem a bit over-simple; however, there's enormous power in just being aware of the intent you are bringing to the moments that matter.

ACTIVITY 2: Fear Setting.

Goal setting is a key to creating an achiever mindset, but what if we applied a similar process to our fears? What if, instead of writing out what we want to happen, we do the complete opposite and describe what we don't want?

It sounds slightly crazy, but a practice called Fear Setting has been used extensively by high performers, from athletes to Wall Street traders and fighter pilots, after it was popularised by Tim Ferriss (2007), author of the *Four Hour Work Week*.

Fear Setting is about facing your fears by specifically listing what you fear and what might happen as a consequence. For example, if you fear being hit all over the field in the final over of a game, then you would list the actual situation (final over, team on verge of win, you get hit for sixes or at least boundaries off every ball) and the consequences (crowd cheering, captain gets flustered, team loses, you feel like you lost the game).

It works for three reasons. First, we tend to underrate ourselves and overrate opponents; second, we overrate the likelihood of a disaster occurring; and finally, in describing the consequences we often find they are bearable or not as bad as we first thought.

If you run a business, you'll just call this "risk management" and wonder why anyone wouldn't think through risks and consequences. However, in sport it's more personal when we confront our own fears.

TOOL 1: Face Your Fears - The Fear Setting Template.

Fear Setting is about facing your fears by specifically listing what you fear and what might happen as a consequence of those fears. Tim Ferriss recommends doing this via a three-page Template which guides the user through four steps outlined in shorter form below. You can download an adapted version from **www.mindfulcricket.com**

Instructions:
Select a fear you would like to address in cricket or in wider life and try out the four steps.

STEP 1: Describe the Fears
Create three lists using the titles below, and put in up to 10–20 entries each.

Define	Prevent	Repair
What are the worst things that could happen?	How do you prevent each from happening?	If the worst happens, how can you fix it?

STEP 2: Identify the Benefits
Make a list of the possible benefits if you are successful or partially successful.

STEP 3: Consider the Cost of Avoidance

Make a list of the costs of your inaction. In other words, if you avoid doing this thing, what might you miss out on?

STEP 4: Reflect and Decide

Take time to read and reflect on what you've written. If helpful, discuss it with a colleague or coach, and then it's up to you to make the decision whether you want to Put It On the Line.

MINDFUL PRACTICE 2: Brilliant Basics.

Dr Atul Gawande wrote the *Checklist Manifesto* (2010), a brilliant book with a scary message about emergency departments. Gawande explained that doctors and nurses know what to do to save the lives of patients with life-threatening conditions like heart attacks and strokes; however, they don't do it consistently and correctly. He painted the picture of a major teaching hospital where a coronary patient has less than a 50% chance of the emergency team administering the right treatment within the critical first 90 minutes.

What he described was what cricket coaches know: **even the best performers forget the basic fundamentals when there's lots happening.** The word "basic" is key.

Gawande's solution was not just breathtakingly simple, but also so effective that it substantially reduced the treatment failures. And in doing so it lifted the performance and safety of emergency and operating rooms around the world. What was the solution? *Checklists* and *Team Check-ins*.

Simple checklists made all the difference to performance. We apply the same approach to cricket and call it "Brilliant Basics".

TOOL 1: Brilliant Basics Checklist.

Brilliant Basics are checklists describing the fundamentals for important activities, such as game preparation, starting an innings and setting up a practice session. Use them to prepare for matches, as a guide to stay on track, or to debrief performance.

Example of a Brilliant Basics Checklist

A useful way to get familiar with the concept and use of Brilliant Basics checklists is to see an example and then create one for an aspect of your game. Below is an example from a club bowler which shows just the minimal Basics. The Player's Journal comments follow.

BRILLIANT BASICS: Starting a Bowling Spell

1.   Loosen up fully

2.   Mark and check run-up

3.   Clear Mind – Centred Breathing

4.   Choose line and length for batters and conditions

5.   Rhythm above all else

6.   Apply Pressure

PLAYER'S JOURNAL

I've found these Brilliant Basics really helpful. Mostly I keep them to 3 or 4 points and have them on cards to use in matches or practice. My focus is definitely better now because this helps Keep It Simple.

Create Your Brilliant Basics Checklist

Decide on a specific activity such as starting your innings and create a Brilliant Basics checklist with up to six points to remind you what is important.

My Brilliant Basics for ...

1.

2.

3.

4.

5.

6.

Many players, coaches and teams use Brilliant Basics checklists for match preparation, or as a quick check-in when the game gets tight. The latter makes sense because it's rarely an exceptional delivery or shot that wins the day, but more often the player who holds their nerve and does the Basics really well.

Practice Tip: Instead of just assuming you will do the right thing under pressure (because you know what to do) use simple checklists and check-ins - applying PDCA - to help you own your space.

MINDFUL PRACTICE 3: Defeat Perfectionism and Comparison.

This practice explores how unrealistic expectations can cause self-sabotage. It is a common issue for players, but one which needs more detail than can be covered in a Workbook. You will find greater depth in the *Mindful Cricket* book, and if this is a concern then chat about it with your Coach or a Psychologist.

Excellence Versus Perfectionism.

There's a fine line between a healthy desire to achieve excellence and perfectionism. The difference is in what drives the behaviour and in the impact on mental and physical wellbeing.

Aiming for excellence is about seeing how good you can be by stretching yourself; the motivation is to explore what's possible. Perfectionism is often driven by avoiding mistakes or failure and seeking the approval (or avoiding the disapproval) of other people.

Three common signs of perfectionism are:

1. Setting impossibly high standards
2. Getting overly upset when making a mistake
3. Distorted view of priorities.

These cause lots of stress and involve hard work. Yet for the perfectionist nothing is ever good enough, which means enjoyment is fleeting at best.

Reflection Questions

Do mistakes make you angry or frustrated?

Do you tend to put more weight on other people's opinions than your own?

Do you often make comparisons with others?

Do you feel driven to prove yourself?

Is there an opportunity to chat with a coach or adviser who could help take off some of that pressure?

ACTIVITY: Tools to Defeat Perfectionism.

Each element of the Game Mindset framework can help to reduce the damaging effects of perfectionism. Here is a brief reminder of some of those practices, and there are more to come in the rest of this Workbook.

Centred Breathing	The Mindful Practices of stillness and Centred Breathing help to reduce the emotional pressure that comes from perfectionistic thinking.
Quieten the Inner Critic	Quietening your inner critic is a sure way to challenge the unrealistic expectations and lack of care for self that is often part of the perfectionist's way of operating.
Go-To-Plans	Simple plans foster a different energy and attention so you can play mindfully, instead of feeling driven to standards that are unrealistic and damaging.
PDCA Loops	The disciplined learning loop of Plan, Do, Check and Adapt helps take away the feelings of being overwhelmed which can arise from perfectionism.
Brilliant Basics	Focusing on the Brilliant Basics is a great way to focus on what you can control, and therefore keep things realistic and achievable.

Are there opportunities to apply these to reduce perfectionism in your game or wider life?

Chapter Takeaways.

Bring a mindset of enjoying the challenges and a desire to test yourself, rather than being fixated on winning and losing. Put It On the Line and be vulnerable by recognising that you aren't defined by winning or losing, but rather by turning up and playing the game.

Jot down your insights from this Chapter:

Quotes from the *Mindful Cricket* book:

Why are we tentative when we'd rather be bold? A primary reason is fear of failure, and particularly fear of being seen to fail or letting others down.

....

Vulnerability is fundamental to Putting It On the Line. It's having the courage to turn up.

....

Even the best performers forget the Basics when under pressure. That's where Brilliant Basics are simply brilliant.

....

Perfectionism takes the fun out of the game and creates tension and anxiety that is counterproductive.

....

CHAPTER 12

Hold The Tension.

3 things you'll gain from this Chapter

1. Understand what causes loss of patience
2. How to see and shape the momentum of a match
3. Skills and tools to Hold the Tension

Match Awareness.

Batsmen fight their way through tough patches, bowlers work to a plan which is overs in the making, and fielders sustain the pressure throughout a long partnership. Cricket rewards those who persevere and stay patient while others throw away the advantage because they couldn't "Hold the Tension."

A key to gaining those rewards is match awareness. That means being alert to the momentum of the game, because it can switch back and forth in less than an over.

Reflection Questions

When have you or your team lost patience and thrown away an opportunity because of not Holding the Tension?

What happened - and are there lessons for you in that experience?

What signs tell you that momentum is shifting in a match?

Would you like to be more effective in creating and using these swings?

MINDFUL PRACTICE 1: Shape the Momentum.

Watch a game of cricket, and observe which team has the momentum at any given moment.

Look for signs such as: the batsmen are stuck on strike, the run rate has slowed, or the fielding team is bringing a lot of energy to the game.

Signs of Batsmen Under Pressure	Signs of Batsmen Holding the Tension
Bogged down	Working the strike by pushing quick singles
Going for big shots	Taking calculated risks
Losing their shape as they overhit the ball	Chipping over the infield

What happens to bowlers in these situations?

Signs of Bowlers Under Pressure	Signs of Bowlers Holding the Tension

Bowlers feeling the pressure often strive harder for a wicket, which causes actions to come unbalanced and rhythm lost. Watch them looking at the footmarks, querying the state of the ball, or just shrugging their shoulders when a slightly false shot is played to a good delivery. They are feeling the pressure!

TOOL 1: Focus on Short-Term Goals.

In any situation where the momentum isn't going your way, a well-chosen short-term goal can provide the focus and confidence you need to persist and stay patient.

Here are some practical ways to build this into practice and match situations:

Use Short-Term Goals to Hold the Tension	
Build the Habit at Practice	Start with setting goals in practice - build them into your Go-To-Plans. Add some examples of your own to the examples for bowling in the list below.
	Bowling Examples: *Set yourself a bowling accuracy target for each six deliveries* *Draw the batsman into a mistimed stroke* *Restrict the batsmen to hitting one side of the wicket.*
Do It in Matches	In match situations get into the habit of setting short-term targets, so they are natural to use when under pressure. Add some examples of your own to the list below.
	Batting Examples: *Break up the field with quick singles* *Get through to the end of the power play* *Move the team in 10-run increments.*

Be deliberate in choosing specific short-term goals to maintain your focus and to shape momentum when the tension is building.

ACTIVITY: Mental Rehearsal: Let Go - Welcome the Squirm.

Visualisation (or mental rehearsal) techniques are widely used by leading cricketers to develop the mindset they need to Hold the Tension in moments that matter.

Instructions:

Make a shortlist of cricket situations where you'd like to be better at Holding the Tension, and then visit **www.mindfulcricket.com** for ideas on visualisation.

> **Practice Tip:** When you get frustrated or angry and lose patience, it's not the situation you are responding to; it's actually your own emotions, which of course are being triggered by your thinking.

MINDFUL PRACTICE 2: Get Above the Noise.

One of the mental skills of people who do well in situations where others are feeling the pressure is the ability to slow things down, quieten the noise and focus on what matters in the moment.

To develop the skill of slowing things down and quietening the noise you need:

- Awareness of how you typically react in these situations
- Acceptance that you can choose to respond differently
- Actions which help to build composure and focus.

You can begin developing that skill with a mindset called "Get in the Grandstand", which simply means getting above the noise and finding the perspective needed to make intelligent choices.

ACTIVITY: Get in the Grandstand.

Instructions:

When we experience setbacks and disappointments on the field of play (or life), it is easy to be caught up in feelings of self-pity, loss and helplessness. However, a mindful approach is to step back, take a breath and think from a different perspective. It's like stepping off the field and taking a few moments to view things clearly from the grandstand.

"Get in the Grandstand" means pausing for a moment, taking a breath and separating yourself from the action and noise. It's the mindful skills we've already covered to slow it down, quieten the noise and reflect: *What's happening here?* and *What's my best choice?*

Give it a try in a situation when you are feeling pressure. Example: *Not scoring early in an innings, or leaking runs in the opening over*

Practice Tip: Sometimes it's very hard to get a detached perspective, so having a coach or friend help you can be a useful strategy. Of course, in the middle of a game you can't ask a coach, but that's where partnerships are so important.

TOOL: Take the Grandstand View on Your Game.

Take a few minutes now to sit in the grandstand and ask yourself these three questions:

Where are you feeling stress or pressure in your cricket or life?

What signs in your thinking or behaviour are signals that you are losing focus, confidence or discipline?

What mindful actions can you take to address this constructively?

Ask for Help.

Whether the tension you feel is coming from sport, study, work or life, it's valuable to have trusted friends or support to help you work through the difficult issues. Coaches, doctors, physical trainers, psychologists and mentors all play this role at times in professional teams.

Being open to sharing your feelings, including doubts and uncertainties, is a doorway to growth and self-confidence, whereas acting out "toughness" is a defensive play which makes you weaker.

What issues would you benefit from discussing with a trusted person?

MINDFUL PRACTICE 3: Defeat Self-Sabotage.

Remember the Brilliant Basics? The reason behind using that tool is the tendency of people to unwittingly self-sabotage their own performances by drifting away from what they know is important.

The causes of this self-sabotage are many and varied; as always, however, awareness is the starting point to check on things like sleep, nutrition, mindful meditation and daily rituals, which can make or break success.

ACTIVITY: Defeating Self-Sabotage.

This activity will help you Get in the Grandstand to identify and defeat any unhelpful habits which might be holding you back and sabotaging your efforts.

STEP 1 Identify the Specific Behaviours	**Are there areas in your life where you are ill-disciplined or self-sabotaging?** *For example, is it nutrition, showing up late, playing get out shots?*
STEP 2 Control Your Environment	**Are you creating the ideal environment for success, or could you be inadvertently creating an environment which encourages self-sabotage?** *For example, if your aim is to stick with good nutrition, then remove the tempting snacks!*

STEP 3	For goals which might be open to ill-discipline and distraction, it can be valuable
Be Accountable	to tell other people your goal. Public commitment increases the chances of
	success because you have more on the line.

STEP 4	Many people just use old-style self-discipline to do what's needed, irrespective of
Get It Done	whether they feel like it or not. As the Nike advertisements says, just do it.
	Are there other areas of self-sabotage where you could simply commit to doing
	the behaviour and/or maintaining the standard?

Chapter Takeaways.

Batsmen fight their way through tough patches, bowlers work to a plan which is overs in the making, and fielders sustain the pressure throughout a long partnership. Cricket rewards those who persevere and show the patience to Hold the Tension.

Jot down your insights from this Chapter:

Quotes from the *Mindful Cricket* book:

The key to shaping the momentum is to Hold the Tension so the game moves in the direction you want.

....

Set and work towards Short-Term Goals to provide focus and build self-confidence.

....

*Be mindful of what you can control, and what just takes away energy
and concentration, and is therefore best to let go.*

....

*When you feel tension building, take a brief pause (breath) to dial down
the "noise" of competition and to think from a different perspective.*

....

Defeat self-sabotage by creating the environment around you which drives commitment and action.

....

Pillar 3.
Play Clever

PILLAR 3: Play Clever.

Cricket is played above the shoulders, and we know that because we watch mindless cricket and see it beaten time and again by cricket smarts. Clever bowling with subtle pressure and variation draws the batsman into a false stroke. Mindless batting overreaches and gets out early on a day when runs were just waiting to be had.

We can learn to play clever cricket. It's not a fixed ability. This is about thinking, and we can sure change that by being aware of our strengths, style and limitations, and by better understanding and reading the game. To Play Clever, let's deep dive into three chapters covering Bat Smart, Bowl Smart, and Keep and Field Smart, where two themes are woven throughout:

Know Your Game

This is playing to your strengths and being aware cricket is a game played inside limitations. It's not the downhill skier on the edge of disaster, but more the Formula One driver holding shape and control while avoiding the overreach.

Read the Game

This is understanding the conditions and the momentum and playing with tactics and pressure in every game situation. It's knowing what to do and when to do it.

Imagine the possibilities when you have a sound foundation of daily habits and rituals built on Brilliant Basics and are ready to bring your strengths to play in the right situation at the right time in the right way.

That's a Mindful Cricketer who knows how to Play Clever.

CHAPTER 13

Bat Smart.

3 things you'll gain from this Chapter
1. Build trust in your batting Basics
2. Learn to Absorb and Apply Pressure
3. Develop your cricket smarts

Playing a Clever Game.

The work you have done on Clear Mind and Play Brave will give you every chance of playing to your potential, but the full benefits come by playing a clever game. That means knowing your game and knowing the game.

Four practices hold the key to smart batting:

Smart Batting Basics	Build trust in your Basics and know how to bring them consistently to your game.
Adapt to Change	Adapt fast to different pitch conditions, and types of bowling.
Create Partnerships	The importance of partnerships and how to use them to gain an edge.
Absorb and Apply Pressure	Applying Mindful Practices to Absorb Pressure, and to flip it back on your opponents.

In this chapter we cover a range of tools to strengthen these four practices. For more detailed coverage, read the *Mindful Cricket* book and join the Mindful Cricket community at **www.mindfulcricket.com**.

Self-Assessment.

Would you like to build greater trust in your batting Basics, adapt faster to changing conditions, forge more successful partnerships, and become adept at Absorbing and Applying Pressure? If the answer is *yes*, then complete the assessment below to identify your strengths and potential areas for improvement.

Instructions:

Reflect on the statements below, one at a time, and use the five-point scale to consider to what extent you agree or disagree.

1 Strongly Disagree **2** Disagree **3** Neither Agree Nor Disagree **4** Agree **5** Strongly Agree

Batting Basics   **Rating**

Most of the time I am confident and consistent in starting my innings

Most of the time I am comfortable in my usual batting position

Most of the time I hold my batting shape

Most of the time I keep my focus on the moment, playing one ball at a time

Most of the time I run well between wickets

Adapting to Change

Most of the time I adapt well to different batting conditions

Most of the time I adapt well to different types of bowlers

Creating Batting Partnerships

Most of the time I am aware of the importance of batting partnerships

Most of the time I communicate well with my batting partner

Absorbing and Applying Pressure

Most of the time I Keep It Simple when batting

Most of the time I Hold the Tension

Most of the time I am alert to opportunities to Apply Pressure when batting

Most of the time I can successfully Apply Pressure when batting

Analysis.

The statements which you have rated 3, 2 or 1 are potential areas for development.

Which areas of improvement will have the greatest positive impact on your cricket?

MINDFUL PRACTICE 1: Smart Batting Basics.

A mindful batsman feels comfortable and confident playing their game in moments that matter such as starting an innings, when momentum shifts, or in the final overs of a close match.

In these moments, it becomes even more important than ever to trust your Basics, because that's what holds things together. Here are five that matter:

BASICS 1: Start Smart with Intent.

Starting Smart is all about consistent, trusted pre-performance rituals, so be sure to get these sorted and make them part of your Brilliant Basics *(see Be Game Ready)*.

A smart start isn't so much about runs, unless your game plan and strengths are suited to all-out attack from the outset; therefore the smartest option is usually to play within your limitations early in your innings.

Take time to assess the conditions and the strengths and limitations of the bowlers. This doesn't mean being passive, it means Playing With Intent in a way that suits your individual style.

Improvement Opportunities?

BASICS 2: Bat Smart in Your Position.

What position in the order do you usually bat? Each position has its own special demands and tactics, which are further influenced by the state of the game.

Opening	Smart openers know the bowlers are fresh, the ball is new, and they'll get some unplayable deliveries. Their intent is to take advantage of gaps in an attacking field by looking for singles, and for boundaries when the opportunity arises.
Number Three	Smart number threes are positive and adaptable in their intent. They'll be mentally ready to bat from the second ball of the game, knowing the role might be to consolidate the team's position and avoid an early collapse, or it could be to build on a strong start.
Middle Order	The smart middle order game is built on partnerships to capitalise on a good start, or to rebuild after the earlier batsmen have been dismissed. Adaptability is also essential, to face a relatively new ball at times, and at other times bat late in the innings when quick runs are needed.
Lower Order	Many matches are won or lost by less than the number of runs scored by the last four batsmen; for this reason alone, Smart Batting means the lower order practise their skills and have the intent to contribute runs, or to defend while a recognised batsman scores.

Reflection Questions

If you open, what's your usual intent in the first 5-10 overs?

If you bat at number three, what intent do you bring?

If you bat in the middle order, how well do you adapt to different situations?

If you bat in the lower order, what intent do you typically bring?

BASICS 3: Hold Your Batting Shape.

The greatest batsman of them all, Don Bradman, practised for countless hours with a stump and golf ball. Not only that, he used a water tank to bounce the ball off. He learned how to shape his body to control a fast and erratic ball. It was an unorthodox technique, yes, but he was sixty percent better than any other player in history. He trusted and held his shape under pressure.

Do you trust yours?

Lose shape and you lose power. Watch batsmen closely to see what happens when they lose their shape. Some fall over slightly to the offside, some reach out too far for the ball, or flick off balance at a wide ball. Another common sight is the batsman caught in "no man's land" against a spinner, neither fully forward nor fully back. They're off balance and vulnerable to a range of possible dismissals.

ACTIVITY: Hold Your Batting Shape.

This activity is a reminder of the importance of setting up your space, and then holding your shape no matter what the conditions.

Instructions:

Get with your coach and agree to work relentlessly on knowing and holding your shape in defence and in forcing shots. Make it your intent to impose your shape on the game.

Stance and Rituals	Be comfortable and settled in your stance and rituals, because that's your space, and owning that is the foundation for your game.
Trust in Defence	Build trust in your defence. Know what a straight bat feels like in your whole body and practise it repetitively, interspersed with some Bradman moves (or the modern-day almost-equivalent, Steven Smith) thrown in to dynamically test your balance when the ball spins, swings, dips or climbs sharply.
Trust in Core Control	Try batting with your feet together and no footwork, so you have to work at holding your middle and upper body shape. It's a good exercise to force you to retain control of your basic shape when hitting balls coming at you in all sorts of different ways.

Mindful Cricket is setting up your space (stance and rituals), trusting your shape and knowing what to do to get it back when things get unbalanced and ragged.

How effectively do you maintain your control over space and shape in a typical innings?

BASICS 4: Bat in the Moment.

Mindful Batting is batting in the moment. It is watching the ball closely and playing, or leaving, according to line and length.

Smart Batting has a rhythm or cadence based on using the regular breaks between deliveries to relax (breathe) and then refocus on the job at hand. Use the 1-2-3 Reset tool as a ritual to minimise the mind drift which affects batsmen once they are settled in.

Do any of these examples suggest you could benefit from developing your ability to bat in the moment?

- Failing to notice changes in field positions
- Playing a lazy defensive shot
- Thinking too much instead of playing the ball on its merits.

BASICS 5: Run Smart.

Being a good judge of a run enables you to apply pressure and reduce pressure. When two batsmen are clear in their decisions and strong in communication, they can run on just about anything. Be alert to the possibility of a quick run. Note the position of the fielders, whether they are right-handed or left-handed, and if they have a strong arm.

Reflection Questions

How clear and decisive is your running between wickets?

Do you spend time practising running between wickets?

Are there regular drills at practice to test your judgement and communication with teammates?

If not, why not?

MINDFUL PRACTICE 2: Adapt to Change.

With all the different versions of the game, pitches, balls, weather and grounds, plus all the variations in types of bowlers, it's no wonder Adapt Fast is a foundation principle of the Game Mindset.

Adapt to Conditions.

Adapting to pitches and ground conditions is essential, yet most of the best international teams still perform much better in their home conditions.

Batting Smart is being mindful of the conditions and what that means to get the percentages in your favour. Do you play most of your cricket on turf or hard wickets? What differences do you experience across these surfaces? What tactics do you bring to these different conditions?

Examples of Tactics:

If the new ball is swinging, then the key is to negate the danger of late swing. Some players bat out of their crease, while others stay back and play as late as possible.

Reverse swing brings slightly different risks, particularly if there is late dip into the stumps. A smart play is to be precise in the angle of your backlift so you don't get trapped playing late and across the line. Also be clear in your intent to get outside the line with definite footwork.

On turning tracks, get the bat out in front of the pad. Quick footwork is essential to avoid losing shape and playing off balance in that halfway position.

Talk with your coach and experienced players to learn their strategies for adapting to different conditions.

With understanding of the Basics, the next step is to set up practice drills to simulate the challenges, and learn strategies that leverage your Basics and work in your favour.

Example of Practice Scenario from *Mindful Cricket* Book:

To prepare their team for a series of games in India, where sharp and at times unpredictable turns were expected, the Coaches set up a series of drills including putting gravel on a practice pitch and throwing into the area so batsmen could practise getting their mindset and technique settled.

By experiencing the unpredictable turn (which replicated the turn from footmarks and worn patches), the batsmen learned to keep a Clear Mind, to stay composed and to work to simple plans.

Initially most reacted by just pushing harder at the ball, but soon they started using their feet, being more confident in sweeping and moving precisely back and forwards. They also learned to focus one ball at a time and to dismiss thoughts of the extreme bounce or spin. Importantly, they came to trust that if they held their shape, those extreme deliveries weren't really a risk.

What practice scenarios can you practise to improve adaptability?

Adapt to Bowlers.

Pitches change, but types of bowling change even more often - and with that come mental challenges and opportunities. Take a few moments to consider your approaches.

Fast Bowling	Bring a Clear Mind, quick reactions, and courage. It's a good test of those Brilliant Basics, so why not create your own checklist?

Swing and Seam	Reduce the potential for movement of the ball, so try tactics that build on your Basics, like getting well forward (often supported by batting just out of the crease), shortening your back lift, leaving anything on a length not bowled at the stumps, and attacking (with shape) any overpitched or short delivery.
Spin	Bring a well-practised defence and agile footwork with a Play Brave–Play Clever mindset. Enjoy the battle, and have an intent to score, while being very positive and definite in defence and in leaving the ball.

MINDFUL PRACTICE 3: Create Partnerships.

Partnerships are one of the most effective ways to gain an edge over the bowling team. When two batsmen stay together and deny the bowlers a wicket, it builds pressure on the bowlers and fielding captain.

Good players and teams recognise the importance of building partnerships, and make it a Brilliant Basic to set team goals while batting.

Watch your teammates' Game Mindset and look for signs when their shape and behaviour shifts. Mid-pitch discussions between overs help, as can words of encouragement or pointing out they are playing outside their game.

Be attentive to your partner and be a team player. It makes your game stronger.

Where are the opportunities to improve your commitment and contribution to batting partnerships?

MINDFUL PRACTICE 4: Absorb and Apply Pressure.

Cricket is such a tactical game that we could fill a complete book on batting tactics alone. That's a lot to take in, but you'll find an ever-growing set of resources at **www.mindfulcricket.com** to help improve your personal and team tactics.

What Does "Absorb Pressure" Mean When Batting?

The pressure you feel when batting is more about your reaction to the situation rather than the situation itself. This is a really important point because if it was about the situation, then everyone would experience the same frustrations, impatience, stress and anxiety, which of course they don't.

Reflection Questions

What situations seem to create excessive pressure for you when batting?

Is it from a dicey pitch, not scoring, playing and missing, chasing a large score, being physically challenged by fast bowling, or deceived by clever swing or spin?

Are there any patterns to when you feel excessive pressure? Does it happen regularly in certain situations, or just occasionally?

Practice Tip: Mindful Batting is knowing that if you stay at the crease things will likely turn in your favour. It is doing things that are constructive, such as looking for singles, regularly discussing options with a batting partner and remaining calm and patient. It is knowing that things will probably not be any easier for a new batsman, so stay composed and persevere with intent.

What Does "Apply Pressure" Mean When Batting?

Batsmen Apply Pressure in a host of ways to bowlers, fielders and captains, but often they don't realise they are doing it and therefore fail to fully capitalise on the situation.

Here are ten ways that come readily to mind:

1.	Take quick singles
2.	Let good deliveries through to the keeper
3.	Hit boundaries early in the over
4.	Chip the ball over fielders
5.	Use the pace of the ball to your advantage
6.	Hold your shape confidently in defence
7.	Show no sign of emotion when you play and miss
8.	Punish poor deliveries
9.	Bat out of your crease, or across in front of off stump to upset line and length
10.	Build a partnership

Mindful Cricket is being aware of how to build pressure in different situations. It's thinking through options, weighing up risk and making decisions.

Take a moment, breathe, and imagine you are batting and want to Apply Pressure. Of course, it depends on the circumstances of the game. However, what are your options?

ACTIVITY: Create Your Own Scenario.

Here is an example of the type of scenario you might use with your team to discuss and share tactics, so you all get better at Applying Pressure in match situations.

Scenario Context

You've just come off the field after a mediocre bowling and fielding effort. The task is 260 to win from 50 overs. The pitch is good although drying and taking some turn, the outfield slow, and opposition attack has a reputation for accuracy over potency. You want to apply the Keep It Simple principle and use PDCA to loop and learn.

Potential Strategies

Plan A might be to get away to a solid start, keep wickets intact, and build the foundation for a launch in the second half of the innings.

Plan B carries more risk and bigger return by going hard in the first six overs while the field is up, and both openers launching an attack on anything short or overpitched.

Let's approach our scenarios in 10-over blocks and look to win or break even on the momentum in each segment.

10 Over Score: 70 for 3

Well above the run rate, but those three wickets mean an extra fielder is staying in the circle and making it more risky to score. What's your twenty over target and the plan to get there?

20 Over Score: 100 for 3

The wicket is starting to turn more, but you've got two batsmen set. They are working the ball around and the energy has dropped a bit in the field. What's your thirty over target, and the plan to get there?

30 Over Score: 140 for 4

A wicket just fell. You've got good batsmen down to at least 9. What's your forty over target and the plan to get there?

40 Over Score: 200 for 6

Good run rate but wickets are falling. What's your plan for the next five overs?

45 Over Score: 235 for 6

The best opposition bowlers will close out the innings. 26 needed off five overs. Do you want to take it down to the wire or go harder earlier?

Chapter Takeaways.

Clever Batting is knowing your game and being match aware, so you can Absorb and Apply Pressure when it's needed. Prepare yourself to be confident in seeking out and playing in moments that matter and you are well on the way to developing the mindset you need to be the best cricketer you can be.

Jot down your insights from this Chapter:

Quotes from the *Mindful Cricket* book:

*Know your shape, trust your shape and know what to do to get your
shape back when things get unbalanced and ragged.*

....

*Understand the conditions and what that means for getting the percentages to go in your favour. Observe
the bowler's actions, grip and field placings. You can learn a lot by being curious and just observing.*

....

Be clear about your intent in defence and attack.

....

Apply Pressure by playing smart cricket. Think through options, weigh up risks and choose the right time.

....

Partnerships are key to Holding the Tension and Playing Smart as a team.

....

CHAPTER 14

Bowl Smart.

3 things you'll gain from this Chapter
1. Build trust in your bowling Basics
2. Learn to Absorb and Apply Pressure
3. Develop your cricket smarts

Trust Your Game.

Bowling is physically different to batting, but the mindset is still about being comfortable and confident to trust your game in moments that matter. Bowlers feel comfortable when they trust their run-up, action and accuracy, while confidence comes from knowing those Basics will hold up pressure, and from variations such as pace, swing and length to outsmart the batsman.

Four practices hold the key to smart bowling:

Smart Bowling Basics	Building trust in your Basics and knowing how to bring them consistently to your game.
Adapt to Change	Mixing up the variations around a solid and reliable stock delivery.
Create Bowling Partnerships	Team plans and working together as a unit.
Absorb and Apply Pressure	Opportunities to Apply Pressure to the batsmen.

In this chapter we cover a range of tools to strengthen these four practices. For more detailed coverage read the *Mindful Cricket* book and join the Mindful Cricket community at **www.mindfulcricket.com**.

Self-Assessment.

Would you like to build greater trust in your bowling Basics, Adapt Faster to changing conditions, forge better bowling partnerships, and become adept at Absorbing and Applying Pressure? If the answer is *yes*, then complete the assessment below to identify your strengths and potential areas for improvement.

Instructions:
Reflect on the statements below, one at a time, and use the five-point scale to consider to what extent you agree or disagree.

1 Strongly Disagree	**2** Disagree	**3** Neither Agree Nor Disagree	**4** Agree	**5** Strongly Agree

Bowling Basics   Rating

Most of the time my first over in a match and in a spell is on line and length

Most of the time I am consistent in executing my intended line and length

Most of the time I hold my bowling shape

Adapting to Change

Most of the time I trust my stock delivery

Most of the time I execute smart and subtle variations

Creating Bowling Partnerships

Most of the time I know the team bowling plans

Most of the time I partner effectively with the other bowlers

Absorbing and Applying Pressure

Most of the time I maintain composure when bowling

Most of the time I have a simple bowling plan

Most of the time I adapt my bowling to suit the momentum of the match

Most of the time I am alert to opportunities to Apply Pressure to batsmen

Most of the time I can successfully Apply Pressure to batsmen

Analysis.

The statements which you have rated 3, 2 or 1 are potential areas for development.

Which areas of improvement will have the greatest positive impact on your cricket?

MINDFUL PRACTICE 1: Smart Bowling Basics.

Bowling is the most physically demanding of the cricket disciplines, and along with these demands comes the message you've heard repeated many times before: it's about doing and trusting your Basics in moments that matter.

BASICS 1: Smart First Over.

Bowlers who aren't mentally or physically ready tend to make one of two fundamental mistakes on their first delivery: either handing the momentum to the batsman by serving up a juicy half volley or half pitcher, or offering sight of their speciality (outswing, leg spin or whatever) instead of making them play. Does this happen to you?

Being a little nervous is to be expected, particularly in the first spell of the game. But don't forget how often a wicket falls soon after a bowling change. That makes it doubly important to get the first few deliveries in good areas with rhythm and zip.

Reflection

What has happened in your first delivery in recent matches?

Have you practised landing your most reliable stock ball first up in every spell at practice?

What's your percentage accuracy? Don't know? Then how can you improve if you don't measure it in some way?

Smart Bowling is dropping quickly into a consistent line and length, and that's a skill that comes from practising in the nets and learning from match experiences.

DRILL: Start Smart Bowling

The starting point for Smart Start Bowling is to get into the habit of bowling in spells in the nets rather than just trundling in one delivery after another.

Plan

Break your bowling into at least three spells at a practice session.

At the start of each spell, aim to accurately land your deliveries with the required speed, flight or zip.

Tell the batsman at the start of each spell you intend to practise dropping quickly into a rhythm and line and length (set yourself a target such as forcing them onto the defensive for those first three deliveries).

Also have a "grid" identified so you know your accuracy.

Do

Be sure to have your Brilliant Basics clear in your mind, so you can trust your delivery each time. Keep It Simple and go with your rhythm.

Check

At the end of six deliveries, check in briefly with the batsman or your coach:

What accuracy did you achieve?

What is the batsman's feedback on your energy (pace, zip, flight)?

Where's the opportunity for improvement?

What's your next goal?

BRILLIANT BASICS CHECKLIST – Start Smart Bowling.

Here's an example of a Brilliant Basics checklist for smart starts to your bowling spells. This is from a First Class cricketer.

Brilliant Basics - Start Smart Bowling

1.	Ask the captain to give an over or more notice
2.	Loosen and stretch using dynamic routine
3.	Mark run-up – and rehearse shape, feel and rhythm through the crease
4.	Roll over one or two deliveries to a teammate
5.	Start with a simple plan (make the batsman play stock ball)
6.	Focus on rhythm and intent

BASICS 2: Line and Length.

Smart Bowling is always about the right line and length for your style of bowling and the conditions, so if there is one Basic to be Brilliant at, this is it!

Many baseball pitchers use a simple three-step approach which has value for bowlers – spot the target, imagine the feel of the pitch, and then go with the feeling towards the target. What they avoid is over-thinking.

Watch a basketballer free throw: Spot, Rehearse Feel, Do It.

The message for cricket? Bowling line and length is about choosing your target area, and then translating that into what you want it to feel like in your body as you move towards the target.

DRILL: Line and Length Test

From time to time give yourself a real challenge by choosing your desired line and length, and measuring your ability to hit the target accurately.

Instructions:
Mark three pitch areas and work with a bowling partner to see who can hit the nominated spot most often while bowling to a batsman.

What score will you get?

Can you imagine a goal kicker in rugby not practising kicking and measuring accuracy? Any tennis player of reasonable standard will know their first and second serve percentages. For some reason, cricket is still way behind other sports in these very basic measures.

> **Practice Tip:** Increasing your awareness of "body feel" will give you more control over the delivery under pressure than just continuing to aim at the target.

BASICS 3: Hold Your Bowling Shape.

Bowling shape is very individual, and very much about body feel and rhythm.

It's the feeling of moving seamlessly through your action and follow-through. It's having your own triggers, such as the twist of the hips for a spinner, flick of the wrist for the seamer, or pulling down the non-bowling arm in the fast bowler.

Lose shape and you lose pace, control and zip. Watch bowlers closely to see what happens when they lose their shape. Some overstride or stumble in their run-ups, some fall away in their action, and others lose momentum by losing energy in their follow-through.

Three Ways to Build Confidence in Your Bowling Shape.

Here are three Basics to build confidence in your Bowling Shape, and an order to approach them:

DRILL 1: Build Trust in Your Delivery Stride

To learn about your shape means getting the feel of your final strides and the delivery itself.
Start without a full run-up so that your full attention is on the feel of the action and follow-through.
Once that's clear, then work your way back to a full run. Give it a try - you'll get more in touch with what your shape feels like than by just pounding away off your full run.

DRILL 2: Build Trust in Your Approach to the Wicket

Know the rhythm and feel of your run-up: *length, strides, pace, body position and entry into the action.*
Know why you run-up. It has only one purpose: to be in position to deliver the ball.
Get comfortable and confident with your run-up and then learn to adapt when bowling with or into a strong wind. Again, it's about the final few steps. Everything else is just for momentum.

DRILL 3: Always Follow Through

The follow-through is your commitment to the action. Without it you are slowing down or not fully completing the delivery.
When Nathan Lyon speaks of "bowling over the top", he's giving clues to what shape means for him and how delivery and follow-through are seamless.

Mindful Cricket is knowing your Bowling Shape and what to do to get your shape back when things get unbalanced and ragged.

> Do you know your Bowling Shape and what to do to get your shape back when things are unbalanced and ragged?

MINDFUL PRACTICE 2: Adapt to Change.

Bowlers don't just adapt to change, they also create it by their array of variations. Fast bowlers have bouncers and yorkers, medium-pacers play with swing and seam, and spinners feast on a banquet of flight and spin options including wrong-uns, doosras, arm balls and flippers.

Most of the top international bowlers I've spoken with believe subtle variations are best because of accuracy and being less obvious to the batsman. They also point to the natural variation of a cricket ball with a seam bouncing off a hard surface, and to the value in having a reliable stock ball to support the variations.

ACTIVITY 1: Do You Trust Your Stock Ball?

A stock ball for quick bowlers is often just short of a length, targeting the top of off stump; for spinners it's a slightly flat delivery turning into a line near off stump; and for medium-pacers a well-pitched ball in the corridor of uncertainty just outside off stump.

> **Reflection Questions**
> What is your stock delivery?
> Does it serve the purpose of building pressure by containing the batsmen?
> How confident are you to deliver it from the first to last delivery of the day?
> Do you have a back-up for different conditions?

It is highly likely that over half the batting team will get themselves out each innings, which suggests there are plenty of wickets to be had from a good stock ball rather than relying on something that swings, seams, dips and hits middle halfway up.

ACTIVITY 2: Developing Your Smart and Subtle Variations.

With a solid stock ball as your basic foundation, start working on two subtle changes which will work in any conditions:

Change in Angle.
Experiment with changes in angle by bowling from close into the stumps and then moving outwards.

Change in Pace.
Vary the pace from slower to quicker deliveries to suit your style of bowling. Be mindful of maintaining rhythm and accuracy so you aren't offering easy runs.

ACTIVITY 3: Ideas for Variations.

Here are some ideas to stimulate your thinking about variations to bring to your game:

1. Medium-Pacers Variation

Deliver three or four deliveries from a metre or so further back than normal while the same batsman is on strike. It will need practice to get the length right, but it has benefits. Bowl your stock ball with the same rhythm and accuracy you normally use. When you have lured the batsman into playing comfortably, begin your run a metre further up, and give them your best swinging or seaming delivery with the same action as used previously. The extra pace and movement from a metre closer will surprise the batsman and give you a great chance of picking up an edge.

Ideas for Variations?

2. Fast Bowlers Variation

A slower ball is a valuable weapon when matched by real pace. Use the slower ball after a couple of quick bouncers, or as the first delivery to a new batsman. Observe the batsmen. Look for players who tend to have their weight back or push with hard hands towards the ball. An accurate, well concealed slower ball might produce a chance in front of the wicket.

Ideas for Variations?

3. Spinners Variation

Accuracy and deception are essential to a spin bowler. If you can, spin the ball, then drop in one that goes straight on, or actually goes the other way (wrong 'un, doosra or arm-ball). Practise this in the nets, with the emphasis on perfecting the delivery first and worrying about concealing it later. Even if the batsman can pick your wrong 'un, they still have to play it.

Ideas for Variations?

The only limit to variations in bowling is your imagination and the ability to bowl them with reasonable accuracy.

MINDFUL PRACTICE 3: Team Bowling.

Consistently restricting batting sides to less than their average requires team bowling, which means a shared bowling plan, commitment from the bowlers operating at any time to synchronise their efforts, and support from fielders.

Team Bowling Plans.

Team bowling plans take the conditions into account, while capitalising on strengths and exploiting the style and limitations of the opposition. The questions to answer in a team bowling plan include:
- What are the pitch and ground conditions?
- What do we know about the strengths, limitation and styles of the opposing batsmen? (eg attacking/defensive)
- What are the strengths and limitations of each of our bowlers?
- How can we work as a team to apply optimal pressure?

Synchronising Efforts.

Effective bowling units give thought to what is going on from both ends and act accordingly. For example, if ten runs come from one over, they keep things tight for an over or two; or if a batsman is struggling against a bowler, they keep them on strike.

Team bowling also means sharing your ideas about batsmen and encouraging other bowlers to do the same. You'll be a stronger player when you are mindful of ways to strengthen the team.

MINDFUL PRACTICE 4: Absorb and Apply Pressure.

The ebb and flow of momentum in a game is a sure sign of how the batting and bowling teams are Absorbing or Applying Pressure.

Throughout the Workbook we've looked at many practices to Absorb and Apply Pressure. Here are a few ideas and reminders to keep building on that momentum.

What Does "Absorb Pressure" Mean When Bowling?

We know pressure is more about mindset than the situation itself, so what sort of situations build pressure on bowlers? I recently posed this question to a Development Squad doing some work on *Absorbing and Applying Pressure.* Here are eight items they identified:

1. Losing the toss on flat, dry pitch
2. Ball not swinging from the start
3. Dropped catches and misfields
4. Quick singles – particularly with left/right batters
5. Fast start – boundaries in opening overs
6. Momentum all with batting team
7. Batting partnerships
8. Not making the batsman play

Reflection Questions

What strategies help you to Absorb Pressure?

What situations still seem to create excessive pressure for you when bowling?

Are there any patterns to when you feel excessive pressure?

What improvements would make a difference to your game?

Practice Tip: In tough situations, slow it down, restrict the damage and get control of the things which you can control. Go back to your Smart Basics (line and length, stock ball, bowling to the field). Remember that no matter the form of the game, two quick wickets are often enough to shift the whole momentum.

What Does "Apply Pressure" Mean When Bowling?

Look no further than the previous chapter, when we discussed the pressures experienced by batsmen, to see the options you have as a bowler to use your stock ball and variations to Apply Pressure.

ACTIVITY: Pressure Opportunities.

This activity has three "pressure opportunities" to consider and exploit in your bowling plans.

Instructions:
Consider the scenarios and Reflection Questions to build awareness of pressure opportunities.

SCENARIO 1: New Batsman
The batsmen want to score. They don't want to be on a duck, and the longer they remain with that zero against their name, the more the pressure builds.

Do you make a point of keeping a player on their duck for as long as possible?

Can you build more pressure early in the innings with field placings?

Are you guilty of giving players easy runs early in their innings?

SCENARIO 2: Fall of Wickets
Cricket is a game of momentum, so a break in a partnership is often the switch that changes the momentum from one team to the other.

Partnerships are the key to batting momentum, so when a new player comes in do you keep them on strike?

How can you use the loss of wickets to pressure the established player?

How disciplined are you in sticking to your plan when wickets are falling?

SCENARIO 3: Chasing a Total

Run chases always present a dynamic between bat and ball. In short form games this can shift very quickly with just a few dot balls, or a couple of sixes.

What strengths do you bring to help Apply Pressure in a run chase?

How effectively do you adapt your bowling to saving runs versus taking wickets?

Do you practise bowling one side of the wicket to restrict the batters?

What are your "go to" deliveries in the final overs?

Chapter Takeaways.

Bowlers feel comfortable when they trust their run-up, action and accuracy. Confidence comes from knowing those Basics will hold up pressure, and from variations such as pace, swing, and length to outsmart the batsman. All of these come from a mindset of Bowling Smart.

Jot down your insights from this Chapter:

Quotes from the *Mindful Cricket* book:

*Smart Bowling is starting smart, and is always about the right line
and length for your style of bowling and the conditions.*

---

*Mindful Cricketers know their Bowling Shape, and they know what to do to
get their shape back when things get unbalanced and ragged.*

---

*Subtle variations are most effective when built on the solid foundation of a good stock
ball (or two) which is bowled accurately without leaking unnecessary runs.*

---

*Consistently restricting batting sides requires team bowling through a shared bowling plan, commitment
from the bowlers operating at any time to synchronise their efforts, and support from fielders.*

CHAPTER 15

Keep And Field Smart.

3 things you'll gain from this Chapter

1. Understand the mindset for good fielding and keeping
2. Strengthen your contribution in the field
3. Develop your "High Catch" mindset

Setting the Team Standards.

Wicket-keeping and fielding are two of the least rewarded aspects of the game, but the standards set behind the stumps and in the field often determine just how successful your team will be. These standards are as much a function of mindset as they are of physical skills. With concentration, backed up by well-practised skills, an ordinary bowling attack can be made to look quite special.

Many of the principles and practices already explored in Bat Smart and Bowl Smart apply equally to Keeping and Fielding, so we won't repeat those points. However, there are some specific ways to bring a Game Mindset onto the field.

Let's begin with the wicket-keeper and their role in Absorbing and Applying Pressure.

How Smart Keepers Apply Pressure.

The keeper, unlike batsmen or bowlers, has a job to do for the whole innings, and they can lift and sustain the efforts of the whole fielding team through their energy and actions.

If you are a keeper, you have at least five essential roles to play over and above your position in the batting order.

140 | Mindful Cricket

ROLE 1: Catcher, Stumper, Stopper.

Your most vital role is catcher, stumper and stopper, because you can make or break the bowlers by capitalising on any chances they create.

Attentive keepers own their space and employ a range of mindset practices like mentally rehearsing stumpings, using resets to switch on and switch off, and breaking the game down into segments with short-term goals.

As a keeper, how effectively do you own your space and hold your shape across a whole innings?

ROLE 2: Leader of the Fielding Effort.

The wicket-keeper is the centrepiece of the fielding effort, handling the ball more often than any other player and getting more catches and run-out opportunities.

Standing behind the stumps also puts you in the ideal position to coordinate the fielding effort, including helping the captain align fielders, directing run-out opportunities, calling for any high catches near the wicket, and recognising fielding efforts. All these actions provide leadership in the field.

As a keeper, how effectively do you provide leadership in the field?

ROLE 3: Adviser to the Bowlers.

From the position behind the stumps, you are in a great position to spot weaknesses in a batsman's technique. You'll also know how each bowler is performing by the feel of the ball hitting the gloves.

Talk with the bowlers and help them to find strategies to remove a particular batsman. If you see a batsman is susceptible to a type of delivery or is getting frustrated, tell the bowler.

As a keeper, how effectively do you work in partnership with the bowlers?

ROLE 4: Confidant to the Captain.

Captaining a cricket team is a challenging task and the captain, like any leader, needs reliable sources of information to make the best decisions.

The keeper is one of the most reliable sources of information for most captains, because they notice when a bowler is losing energy or becoming a little inaccurate - often before it becomes obvious to the captain.

Have you established a trusted relationship and good communication with the captain?

ROLE 5: Appealing and Chatting.

An enthusiastic appeal from the keeper and bowler seems to increase the chances of a positive umpiring decision, so the keeper has a key role to play in bringing that energy when chances occur.

As a keeper, you'll also be expected to sustain the "chatter" in the field, and possibly towards the batsmen.

What's your thinking about constantly chatting with, or about, the batsmen in between deliveries, as a way of trying to distract their concentration?

How Do We Rate A Keeper?

A wicket-keeper doing their job well is often not noticed, which means the keeper needs to be proficient at assessing their own performance.

Learning to do this to the point where it becomes a habit can help you to sustain and lift your own performance standards and impact as a keeper.

My suggestion to most keepers is to create their own Brilliant Basics checklist to use as a debriefing tool to review their performance.

ACTIVITY: Create A Brilliant Basics Checklist.

This activity is recommended for wicket-keepers, to help them create a template for use when preparing for and debriefing match performances.

Create Your Brilliant Basics Checklist for Wicket-Keeping

Make a list of the keeping activities and actions you feel are most important in preparing for a match and in the match itself. For example, your list might include pre-game routines, and in-the-game activities such as footwork, watching the ball, staying down to spinners, focusing in the moment, encouraging the fielders, maintaining composure and catching technique.

My Brilliant Basics

1.

2.

3.

4.

5.

6.

Use your list as a Brilliant Basics checklist in preparing for matches and when debriefing your performance. For the debrief choose a rating scale such as points out of ten, where a rating of one means very poor and ten means excellent.

Smart Fielding Applies Pressure.

"Fielding Smarts" are a combination of the mindset skills you've learned from batting and bowling plus technical skills such as fielding ground balls, taking catches and throwing.

Alert, enthusiastic and committed fielding Applies Pressure, and can make even an average bowling team look very good.

Reflection Questions

What mindset and attitude do you bring to your fielding?

Do you focus in the moment and treat it as enjoyable and a challenge?

Or do you just go through the motions, often distracted, and treat it as something that has to be done?

Make Mindset Matter to Your Fielding.

Good fielders I've worked with seem to have four common practices which you can easily bring into your practice and match rituals.

1. Treat fielding as an enjoyable challenge with high standards.

Mindful Cricket is enjoying fielding and setting high standards across the whole innings and in circumstances that can be unpredictable and high-pressure. Good fielders often set themselves little challenges, like causing confusion in the running between wickets, or even keeping score on how many runs they've saved and making it a competition with a teammate.

How can you create small challenges to make your fielding mindset more alert?

2. Use a 1-2-3 Reset ritual.

The key to fielding concentration is to relax between deliveries and then to call up concentration when needed. Like batting, this requires a ritual or routine using some form of 1-2-3 Reset.

What rituals or routines do you use to reset concentration?

3. Use mental rehearsal.

Fielding can also be made more enjoyable by simple visualisation and mental rehearsal skills. Every few minutes imagine that a catch has been hit your way; see yourself taking the catch, and pay attention to the feel of the catch. This simple technique has been used by slip fielders for years.

Are there opportunities to build mental rehearsal into your fielding approach?

4. Develop a "High Catch" mindset.

How often do you hear a teammate say, "If I get a catch, I hope it's a reflex one"?

Players often prefer catches which don't allow them time to think about it; however, to be effective and enjoy your fielding it is important to build a sound, comfortable and reliable physical and mental technique.

That mental technique needs to create a relaxed confident approach rather than the "not wanting to drop the ball" mindset which means tighter muscles, "harder hands" and consequently less chance of success.

The drill below is recommended.

High Catch Mindset.

Work with your coach or teammates on an oval to practise the mindset which goes with catching a high ball.

Plan

Begin by thinking through the routine that you want to go through once you have sighted the ball. This routine needs to be very simple and should involve nothing more than positioning yourself and your hands, watching the ball and anticipating the feeling of giving with your hands as the ball arrives.

Make this your Brilliant Basics checklist, and be sure to build in Composure, Focus and Keeping It Simple. Above all, go with the attitude of enjoying the challenge.

Do

Work on different types of catches (short, medium and long catches at different heights). Also set the rhythm of the session (time between catches) so you increasingly replicate match conditions.

1. Start with easier catches to get your routine right
2. Dial up the difficulty
3. Add challenges such as facing away until the ball is hit up for a high catch
4. Create a high catch challenge, which means everyone comes out a few times in the session and just gets one catch. It's a good way to simulate the game situation

Check

Build in regular debriefing to reflect on:

1. *How solid is your technical routine and technique?*
2. *Is the Brilliant Basics checklist working for you?*
3. *What mindset is helping or hindering your approach?*
4. *What simulations/game sense drills will help to build confidence in match conditions?*

Adapt

Apply what you have learned, so you will improve.

Field Smart in Your Position.

Each position has its own demands. Here are some prompts to reflect on your game and areas to improve:

Slips and Gully

To be a good slip and gully fieldsman means taking the predictable catches as well as the ones that come out of the blue. This comes from well-practised reflexes, supported by good concentration and self-confidence (built on reset rituals).

Improvement opportunities?

Close to the Wicket	To succeed as a close-in fielder requires excellent concentration skills, courage and judgement. The ability to stay low, anticipate catches and go for cover at the right time are fundamental.
	Improvement opportunities?
Outfield	The outfield positions include fine leg and deep third man, together with many forward-of-the-wicket positions. Your ability to quickly pick up the line that the ball is taking, move speedily to gather the ball, and dispose of it quickly and accurately are key.
	Improvement opportunities?
The Infielder	The infield includes cover, square leg, point and mid-wicket, mid-on and mid-off. As an infielder you will be walking in with the bowler ready to pounce on the ball if it is hit in your direction, and looking to create run-out opportunities. Backing up is also a key.
	Improvement opportunities?

Chapter Takeaways.

Setting and sustaining high standards in the field is fundamental to Mindful Cricket. Whether your role is wicket-keeper or fielder (in any position), you can play a key part in the success of your team and add to your enjoyment and performance by developing the Game Mindset.

Jot down your insights from this Chapter:

Quotes from the *Mindful Cricket* book:

The standards set behind the stumps and in the field often determine just how successful your team will be.

....

As wicket-keeper you are the centrepiece of the fielding effort, handling the ball more often than any other player and getting more catches and run-out opportunities.

....

Alert, enthusiastic and committed fielding Applies Pressure, and can make even an average bowling team look very good.

....

The key to good concentration while fielding is to relax between deliveries and then to call up concentration when needed.

....

Pillar 4.
Play Better

PILLAR 4: Play Better.

Play Better is about learning and adapting, to be the best you can be.

This pillar builds on the Adapt Fast principle and practices (including PDCA), and introduces three other principles which feature strongly in the Game Mindset of players who do well over long periods of time:

- Growth Mindset
- Be Game Ready
- Bring Optimism.

Growth Mindset is the belief that talent and ability aren't fixed, so you can improve in anything you put your mind to. Be Game Ready will help you to create your pre-game and pre-performance routines and rituals. Bring Optimism will show you how your mindset has a filter which can be set to optimistic or pessimistic, and what a huge difference that can make to confidence, composure and openness to learn and grow.

Play Better is a great reminder that we all have the capability to improve and can build that capability through strengthening our mindset and thinking.

CHAPTER 16

Apply A Growth Mindset.

3 things you'll gain from this Chapter
1. Assess whether you are using a Growth Mindset
2. Improved skills in receiving feedback
3. Understand the value of self-care

Don't Believe It.

Cricket is a sport where great players are revered as having God-given talent, and judgements on all others seem to go straight to unchangeable limitations:

He can't make runs on seaming pitches. She can't bowl long spells. He just can't play the short ball. Players at Test level don't need coaching. You're either good enough, or you're not once you reach this level.

This is Fixed Mindset. Every statement above has one underpinning belief: players have fixed limits. Perhaps they do, but few come even close to reaching them.

Don't Believe the Negativity.

The research of Stanford University Psychologist Carol Dweck (2008) has proven that talent and abilities aren't just genetic traits fixed in place. Work hard, learn and you will improve and be more successful.

Not Yet.

Growth Mindset is believing in the power of learning and growing. Ironically, it's about failure.

It's about having the curiosity, courage and desire to push out of the comfort zone which protects you with beliefs such as: "I'm just not good at maths, hook shots, bowling into a strong wind, talking to groups, etc etc."

If that's your mindset, you are thinking in terms of "pass or fail" instead of "not yet." Cultivating a "not yet" attitude to cricket and life sets you up to learn and develop, rather than being restricted by beliefs that simply aren't true.

Self-Assessment: What Mindset Do You Bring?

This brief but powerful self-assessment asks you to think about the mindset you bring to challenges and your own growth and development.

Instructions:

Reflect on the items in the table below. Which of each pair is most like you?

I go towards risks and challenges	<->	*I avoid risks and challenges*
I think about strengths first	<->	*I think about weaknesses first*
I bounce back from setbacks	<->	*I get knocked off track by setbacks*
I'm open to failing and getting feedback	<->	*I don't react well to failure or feedback*
I take care of my body and mind	<->	*I take my body and mind for granted*

Insights?

Three Growth Mindset Strategies.

No one has either a Fixed or Growth Mindset. There will be times where you bring a Growth Mindset and other times when a Fixed Mindset emerges. For example, when you are tired or feel overwhelmed, a Fixed Mindset might show through, whereas in the Blue Zone you might notice Growth Mindset at play.

The key question is whether you can switch on Growth Mindset when it matters, and I've consistently seen three strategies used successfully by cricketers to do this.

MINDFUL PRACTICE 1: Strengths First.

It is easy to drift into a negative spiral when things aren't going as well as we'd like.

When that happens, have you noticed your focus goes towards your weaknesses? That then brings out the unhelpful critic who wants nothing more than to make you feel better by avoiding things and playing a lesser game.

Stop that thinking. Replace it with a "strengths first" mindset, and begin that by developing a Strengths Portfolio.

ACTIVITY: Create A Strengths Portfolio.

This activity encourages you to identify and record key strengths in your game, and might help you to further build on the Go-To-Plan library in Keep It Simple.

Instructions:
Reflect on the following points:

People have different strengths, and no one is good at everything.

What strengths do you currently have in cricket?

Our strengths change over time as do our expectations of what a strength means.

What could you do differently to better use and develop these strengths?

Doing things we are good at increases energy and motivation.

What strengths do you want to have in one year from now?

Allow yourself time to genuinely reflect on the answers in each area.

What's one thing you could do to really make "strengths first" your mindset?

MINDFUL PRACTICE 2: Find and Receive Challenging Feedback.

Without feedback you can't learn. However, some feedback stings, so it's no wonder many players go out of their way to avoid it.

How do they avoid it? By ignoring it, not taking risks, denying they were really trying, or by being defensive or aggressive towards the person offering the feedback.

Why Feedback Stings.

Challenging feedback presses emotional buttons. A coach or another player might say you aren't up to performing in the big games. Ouch. You might feel the need to defend yourself, but pause for just a moment. Ask yourself whether it is more important to prove how good you are now, or to speed up your development. If it's the latter, then feedback is essential.

ACTIVITY: Get the Most from Feedback - The 3Rs.

Next time you get some challenging feedback, resist the urge to react immediately and instead try **The 3Rs: Receive, Reflect, Respond**.

Here are the steps for each:

Receive	Receive the feedback by showing you are open to it. Take a Centring Breath, then show it in your body language, in the way you listen and are curious to learn. In the first few seconds only say "thank you", then move to the next "R".
	What's been your usual reaction to challenging feedback?
Reflect	Reflect means to pause (breathe) and think about what you've been told, separate the emotion from the message, and take time to choose what is of value to you and your goals. Not all feedback is going to be useful or accurate, so if it's hard to get perspective by yourself, ask a coach or friend to help you reflect.
	Could you be better at reflecting on the messages in the feedback to get the value?
Respond	Respond by taking action. That might mean asking for more feedback or experimenting with new approaches to address the issues in the feedback.
	When have you acted on feedback, and when have you let the opportunity pass?

Practice Tip: Use the 3Rs whenever you receive feedback, so you get the most value while also encouraging people to continue offering it.

Find Quality Feedback.

We all need valuable feedback to help reinforce our strengths and to give us insights on areas that need improvement. What you do with that feedback is your responsibility, but it's essential to get quality feedback from people you respect.

Who comes to mind when you think about "non-sugar-coated" and valuable feedback?

MINDFUL PRACTICE 3: Take Care.

This final strategy is perfectly explained in this brief but compelling journal of an international player, which is extracted from the *Mindful Cricket* book.

> *Credit where credit is due. I was on a fast track to wrecking my career until one of the Academy Coaches got me to have a chat with the Performance Psych Coach. I was training and competing every minute of every day. I didn't do recovery or any of the mindful stuff because I thought I was tough enough to not need it. Instead, I tried to win everything at training, taking more wickets, hitting the ball further and always being at the front of any runs or gym work.*
>
> *I started getting physical niggles in my back and hamstring, so I just did more stretching and went through the pain. Then the coaches took me aside and said my teammates thought I wasn't a team player. I told them it wasn't about making friends. I was in this to be the best. If people didn't like it, well, bad luck.*
>
> *They dropped me, and at the same time I was diagnosed with a stress fracture.*
>
> *Cut a long story short: The Psych helped me extract my head from you know where. I started taking care of myself and showing some care and respect for others. He called it "Take Care". It's why I'm now a successful professional cricketer and not a broken wreck.*

Taking care of yourself is important, but it is a message easily forgotten when you are busy and occupied with day-to-day demands. Of course, you can't expect to sustain high levels of performance without giving attention to "fuelling your mind and body."

Self-Assessment.

This activity introduces the concept of self-care, and provides a basic checklist to reflect on five items which are all about building and sustaining the energy and focus which sit at the centre of Mindful Cricket.

Instructions:

Consider each of the items below and rate whether it is something you are doing well or there is need to improve. Give yourself a score out of 10 (1 = Poor; 10 = Excellent). Ignore any items that aren't important to you.

Rating

Physical Wellbeing (sleep, nutrition, stretching, hydration)

Emotional Wellbeing (rest, relaxation, balance, calmness)

Intellectual Wellbeing (learning, stimulation)

Relationship Wellbeing (trust, connections)

Spiritual Wellbeing (faith, connection)

How are you constructing your days and weeks?
Are you taking care of yourself, and looking after your most important asset?

Making the Three Strategies Work for You.

The three strategies for Growth Mindset provide a compelling insight into the difference between Growth and Fixed Mindset.

It starts with the simple phrase "not yet", and from there you have all the skills and resources to build it into your Game Mindset.

Are you bringing a Growth Mindset or a Fixed Mindset to your cricket?

Are you aware of things which push you towards a Fixed Mindset at times (eg tiredness, challenging feedback)?

Is there one action you could take to strengthen your Growth Mindset?

What benefits would you hope to gain from doing that?

Chapter Takeaways.

Talent and abilities aren't just genetic traits fixed in place. Growth Mindset is believing in the power of learning and growing. Ironically, it's about failure. Work hard, learn, and you will improve and be more successful. Are you consistently bringing that mindset to your cricket and other important areas of life?

Jot down your insights from this Chapter:

Quotes from the *Mindful Cricket* book:

Instead of "Pass or Fail", think "Not Yet."

....

Strengths First: Focus on strengths not weaknesses, avoid making excuses, and challenge the self-defeating thinking which is anchored in the past and doesn't define your future.

....

Find Challenging Feedback: Focus on how fast you are developing and not on how good you are. Welcome feedback by using the 3Rs: Receive, Reflect, Respond. It's your choice.

....

Take Care: Protect your most important asset - you!

....

CHAPTER 17

Be Game Ready.

3 things you'll gain from this Chapter

1. Build the daily habits that bring out the best you
2. Create an effective pre-game routine
3. Build consistency into your game

Good Habits.

Want to perform more consistently near your best as a cricketer? Then build consistency into your daily habits or rituals, because the way you organise and conduct yourself during the week has a direct and lasting impact on the way you play on the cricket field.

To build that consistency we focus on two Mindful Practices:

Daily Habits	Noticing and learning what makes you feel energised and what makes you feel flat, so you can build habits that bring out your best
Pre-Game Routine and Rituals	Extending your daily habits into pre-game routines and rituals that help you to be mentally and physically prepared to perform

Practice Tip: It is close to impossible to be disorganised and inconsistent all week and then bat or bowl in a disciplined way for hours in matches. Set the foundation for your game in your daily habits and then bring them into your pre-match preparation.

MINDFUL PRACTICE 1: Build Your Daily Habits.

Good daily habits in the form of "little rituals" help to build confidence and composure instead of the reactivity that comes from being externally driven and distracted by pressures and distractions. Four habits in particular have real value for cricketers.

HABIT 1: Optimal Hydration.

Dehydration is a primary cause of low energy and poor focus. Over 60% of your body weight is water, so not surprisingly every cell, tissue and organ depends on water to operate effectively. Without enough water, waste accumulates, temperature rises, joints stiffen and tissues are more susceptible to damage. If you are at all dehydrated, there will be no Clear Mind.

ACTIVITY: Test Your Hydration.

My business and sport clients often report that just one week of experimenting with how water impacts their mind and body reduced the tiredness, slight headaches and lack of focus they were experiencing in the afternoon.

The amount of water you need depends on age, exercise, humidity, body weight, health and so on; so it's best to experiment.

Why not experiment with hydration for a week, and see what you observe and learn?

HABIT 2: Stretch, Loosen and Recover.

A daily ritual of stretching is close to a "must do" for any high performer. Whether that means yoga, foam rollers or general stretching, it is all about what makes you feel and perform at your best. Add to that whatever helps you to recover from training or stress, such as sauna, showers, a walk on the beach or in nature etc, and you are taking care of your greatest asset - you!

These rituals set the foundation for your pre-game warm-up, which is essential for mental and physical preparation.

ACTIVITY: Set Your Stretch, Loosen and Recover Rituals.

What activities help you to stretch and loosen to feel and perform at your best? How do you recover from training and the daily stresses of life? Are there stretching, loosening and recover rituals you can build into your daily life?

HABIT 3: Pacing for Pressure.

We all have a natural pace or cadence. What's yours? Do you like to do things fast, or is your drumbeat slower and more methodical? What happens to your pace and thinking when you're under pressure?

As pressure builds, most people notice three things happening:

Thoughts and actions speed up	They move faster, jump from one thing to another and react quickly to whatever happens
Noise in their mind increases	There are more thoughts, more issues to handle, more options to consider, which make it appear more complicated
Focus shifts to the consequences	The imagination comes into play and wonders what will happen in the future - what if?

Clever cricket is doing the opposite of these three practices:

- Instead of speeding up, slow it down;
- Instead of adding to the noise, quieten it down; and
- Instead of allowing mind drift towards the consequences, focus on one ball at a time.

What do you observe about your pace? Are there strengths or improvement opportunities?

ACTIVITY: Use Daily Pressures to Control the Pace.

One of the most effective ways to train yourself to control the pace when things seem to be speeding up is to capture the opportunities every day to slow it down, quieten it down, and focus on one step at a time.

Here are a few reminders and ideas to guide you on these three Brilliant Basics:

Slow It Down	Reduce reactivity by putting short pauses between activities in your day, and in your reaction to distractions. Instead of grabbing for your device when you leave a meeting or as soon as it pings, pause for a moment, take a Centring Breath and then respond.
Quieten the Noise	Notice when your thoughts are becoming jumbled or you are making a situation bigger than it needs to be. That might be when you are stuck in a traffic jam or frustrated by someone's behaviour. Take an intentional breath to quieten the noise and set a short-term goal.
Ball-By-Ball	Catch yourself whenever you are trying to do two things at once, or worrying about the future instead of focusing on the now. Be deliberate in focusing on one thing. Give it your attention, whether it's a conversation, study or cleaning your home. Practise compartmentalising and you'll do better under pressure.

HABIT 4: Set Up to Suit Yourself.

Do you waste time or energy in your day-to-day life because of lack of clear priorities or distractions? What causes these lapses?

The answer might lie in the structure of your day and the environment you create around you.

Reflection Questions

How do you currently structure your day?

What sort of waking, rest and sleep routines work best for you?

What set-up of tools and physical layout suits you?

Practice Tip: When we look at your pre-game rituals in a moment, it's unlikely they'll be any more effective than the way you structure your day and create an environment around you.

ACTIVITY: Test Your Set-Up.

Instructions:

Reflect on the way you organise your day, and the tools and resources you use to bring comfort and focus.

Example:

I travel most weeks, which means well over 100 plane flights a year and plenty of different environments. Accordingly, I have a range of simple habits, rituals and equipment to help me perform and relax anywhere, anytime. This includes songs on my smartphone, earphones and a backpack with items like keys, pens, laptop and snacks with easy access. I have Evernote on my phone and laptop to keep important information, a Kindle to read novels and business books, and travel lists to ensure minimal time and maximum accuracy in packing.

Insights

Are there opportunities to subtly improve your waking, rest and sleep routines? What set-up of tools and physical layout of your work or study spaces can be redesigned to suit you better?

MINDFUL PRACTICE 2: Create Your Pre-Game Routine and Rituals.

Mindful Cricket is about performing consistently, and one of the most reliable ways to create consistency is good preparation. Pre-game routines and rituals will help you to do that and they will mostly be an extension of your daily habits.

ACTIVITY: Design Your Game Readiness Plan.

The following four steps build on the awareness you gained from exploring the Zone, and from experimenting with daily habits. They will help you design a pre-game routine with rituals that get you into optimal physical and mental shape. A detailed guide is also available at **www.mindfulcricket.com.**

STEP 1: Know What "Game Ready" Means.

Think about the matches coming up and ask yourself:

....

If I was totally ready to perform at my best...

....

Mentally: *What would I be thinking?*

Emotionally: *How would I be feeling?*

Physically: *What shape would I be in?*

Environmentally: *What set-up would I create?*

STEP 2: Assemble the Pieces.

Think back over the past season to matches when you felt most comfortable and in control of your game from the start.

What did you do to create the environment where you were
mentally, physically and emotionally set up to succeed?

Here are some prompts to stimulate your thinking:
- What were your habits and rituals in the week leading up to the game?
- How did you practise?
- Did you think about the game a lot or a little?
- What helped you to be physically energised?
- What attitude did you bring?
- What warm-up and final preparation did you do?
- How did you deal with distractions or "noise"?

Practice Tip: Aim to keep it as simple as possible and don't be concerned if you aren't sure, because this is a starting point to build on.

STEP 3: Draft Your Game Readiness Plan.

Start a week out from the game, and draft a plan describing the behaviours and set-up you want to include in your Pre-Game Rituals. Here is an example:

When	What and How
Weekly	Set your goals and plan for the week, including reviewing the opposition and the likely conditions.
	What are your key themes for the week?
Daily	Commit to your daily habits including daily hydration, stretching, sleeping, mindfulness and cricket practices.
	What is needed to feel organised and in control?
Day Before	Get organised with gear and define your Go-To-Plan.
	Will it be helpful to schedule quiet time for centring or mental rehearsal?
Morning	Follow your usual pre-match routine of meal, stretch, visualising and do some reflex catches.
	Do you have a Brilliant Basics checklist for this?
Warm-Ups	Get involved at your ideal pace in the stretching and building up to full load. What pace will you bowl at?
	What throwdowns will be helpful? Any reflex catching?
In Game	Have equipment ready and use your Go-To-Plans to Keep It Simple and focused.
	What's important to remember about your mindset in match situations?

STEP 4: PDCA Your Plan.

To refine your Game Readiness Plan, use the PDCA structure to guide your thinking.

Plan

When and how are you going to begin using the plan?

Do

Give it a go, because it's only as good as the value you get from doing it.

Check

Reflect on what worked, what didn't work, and what needs changing.

Adapt

Adjust the plan and PDCA again.

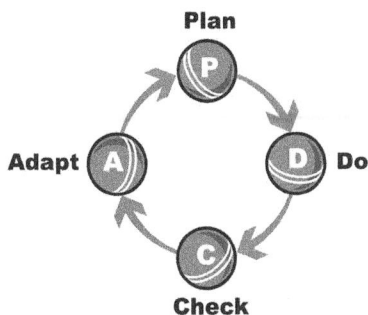

Practice Tip: Use the PDCA loop so you continuously improve from one experience to the next. The power of regular Plan, Do, Check and Adapt is proven across so many areas of life.

Chapter Takeaways.

Game readiness starts with the way you organise and conduct yourself during the week. Your game readiness routine and rituals then become an extension of these habits, which makes them much more reliable under pressure.

Jot down your insights from this Chapter:

Quotes from the *Mindful Cricket* book:

Good daily habits in the form of "little rituals" build a sense of confidence and security,
while also laying the foundation for building the all-important pre-game rituals.

....

Capture the countless opportunities every day to slow down, quieten down, and focus one step at a time.

....

Mindful Cricket is about performing consistently, and one of the most
reliable ways to create consistency is good preparation.

....

Create and continually refine your pre-game routines and rituals to help
you to be in the optimal mental and physical state to perform.

....

CHAPTER 18

Bring Optimism.

3 things you'll gain from this Chapter

1. Know when pessimism is damaging your game
2. How to develop a more optimistic mindset
3. Choosing the changes you want to make to your mindset

What's Your Filter?

Just as a camera takes different pictures depending on the filter over the lens, we see the world differently depending on the filters we use.

One of the most impactful examples is the difference between an "optimistic filter" and a "pessimistic filter". The latter can be heard when players say things such as:

I never bowl well into the wind. I can't bowl to left-handers. Why am I bowling from this end? If I get the edge, they'll probably drop the ball anyway.

With a pessimistic filter, our mind is focused towards difficulties, barriers and weaknesses; and it is proven to create players who are less confident, more stressed, and lower performing.

Self-Assessment.

Reflect on the items in the table below. Which of each pair is most like you?

Stresses over a poor shot	*<->*	*Resets to play the next ball well*
Assumes losing the toss is a disaster	*<->*	*Has a plan to put pressure on opponents*
Expects bad things to happen	*<->*	*Keeps working to make good things happen*
Ignores little things that go well	*<->*	*Seeks small victories*
Blames the umpire	*<->*	*Accepts poor decisions and moves on*
Shows negative reactions to opponents	*<->*	*Projects positive body language*
Remembers bad shots or deliveries	*<->*	*Remembers good shots or deliveries*
Unwilling to try new things	*<->*	*Willing to try new things*

Insights

Clearly, the column on the left is a pessimistic mindset, while the right is much more optimistic. What situations push you towards the left? How much better is your enjoyment and performance with an optimistic mindset?

Developing Your Optimism.

An optimistic frame of mind can be learned and strengthened by applying simple mindful activities and tools to cricket challenges.

Three practices hold the key to strengthening your optimistic filter:

Change your Filter	Be more aware of your mindset and the opportunity to choose a more optimistic filter.
Choose Optimistic Language	Understand how the words you use in thinking and speaking play a big part in your overall attitude and self-confidence.
Be Grateful	Pause to reflect on what's working and what's valuable in your life, rather than dwelling on what's not.

Spiral or Springboard?

A player with an optimistic filter believes there are possibilities, and avoids the negative pessimistic spiral which describes one of the golden rules of sport psychology:

....

Our own mistakes and our opponent's good luck have much less impact on whether we achieve our goals than what we do immediately after it happens.

....

ACTIVITY 1: Change Your Filter.

The essential first step in developing a more optimistic filter is lifting your awareness of when you experience a "mind drift" towards the pessimistic. It is then your opportunity to do something about it.

Your Task
Be alert to those times when uncomfortable emotions such as frustration, anger or disappointment are creeping into your game and affecting your mindset. Don't obsess over every thought; just pause when you notice, and follow these four steps:

STEP 1	When you sense the uncomfortable feelings, just take note of what you are doing. *For example, you might be bowling to a batsman who is on top, or be waiting to bat.*
STEP 2	Describe the feeling. *For example, you might describe it as getting frustrated or feeling anxious and on the verge of panic.*
STEP 3	Observe how your thinking and actions are changing. *For example, getting down on yourself for making errors and losing intent and shape.*
STEP 4	Intentionally bring your thinking back to being more optimistic by using a Mindful Cricket tool. *For example, do a 1-2-3 Reset, or use your Go-To-Plan.*

When can you use this approach to shift from pessimism to optimism?

ACTIVITY 2: Choose Optimistic Language.

When thinking or speaking, the words or phrases you use directly impact your mindset and performance. Words like "never", "can't" and "yes but" can be self-defeating and set up a pessimistic filter which makes you sound and feel less powerful and less able to find possibilities.

Your Task

Reflect on the questions below, and in your day-to-day life be alert to how you talk about the challenging situations you face. Some players get quite a breakthrough in their mindset when they realise the words they use are more "critic" than "coach".

What language do you use when discussing an upcoming game?

Is it more optimistic or pessimistic?

What language do you use when devising a plan?

Do your sentences start with: "I can ..." and "I will...", or "I hope" and "I'll try"?

Are you more likely to say "yes and..." or "yes but..." ?

How does this affect your mindset?

Practice Tip: To generate a more confident and composed mindset, replace the pessimistic words and phrases with sentences starting with: "I can", "I will...", and "Yes and..." Have plans that describe what, how and when you will do things.

ACTIVITY 3: Be Grateful.

It's so easy to take for granted all the good things in our lives and to become absorbed in the one or two things that aren't going our way at the time.

Many people challenge and change this habit through a daily ritual of writing down three things for which they are grateful. How about giving it a try?

Each day write down **three things** for which you are grateful. They might include important relationships, opportunities you have, or your own health and fitness. It doesn't matter if the same things repeat themselves. Ideally combine this activity with centring, because jotting down the grateful list and then centring or meditating can be a very effective Mindful Practice.

Day 1

Day 2

Day 3

Day 4

Day 5

Day 6

Day 7

Many players have told me this exercise helped them to put things into better perspective, which reduced feelings of pressure and increased confidence. That's a recipe for finding the Blue Zone!

Any insights?

Bringing a More Optimistic Filter.

Take a few minutes to consider the Reflection Questions, which address the key topics we've covered in this brief introduction to bringing an optimistic filter to your game and life.

Reflection Questions

Are you more naturally optimistic or pessimistic?

Is your current frame of mind helping or hindering your focus and execution of the game skills?

What thoughts and feelings cause mind drift towards the pessimistic?

What "early signals" might help you to spot when you are becoming pessimistic?

Is there an opportunity to use reframing more often in your day-to-day life?

Chapter Takeaways.

You can face the same situation and have two completely different experiences because of the way you interpret that situation. If you see it through a pessimistic filter, you see difficulties and feel less powerful because things seem more permanent and all-pervasive. However, with an optimistic filter you view setbacks as temporary, and look for possibilities. Not surprisingly, your mental health and wellbeing can change just by changing the filter.

Jot down your insights from this Chapter:

Quotes from the *Mindful Cricket* book:

Just as a camera takes different pictures depending on the filter over the lens, we see the world differently depending on the filters we use.

....

If we bring a "pessimistic filter", chances are we'll be less confident, more stressed, and lower performing than if we choose an "optimistic filter".

....

Our own mistakes and our opponent's good luck have much less impact on whether we achieve our goals than what we do immediately after it happens.

....

Choose language and actions which reinforce an optimistic mindset. Be grateful.

....

Part D.

IMPLEMENTING THE GAME MINDSET FRAMEWORK

In this final section of the *Mindful Cricket Workbook*, we bring together the pillars, principles and practices to set you up to implement this for yourself, your team or your club.

This section is intentionally brief because the content and approach continues to adapt and grow as our Mindful Cricket community creates and shares ideas and tools to bring the Game Mindset to life. For the most up-to-date information on tools, drills and applications, or for online coaching and support, visit **www.mindfulcricket.com**.

CHAPTER 19

The Mindful Cricket Pathway.

3 things you'll gain from this Chapter

1. Recap of the key elements of Game Mindset
2. Five-step plan to implement Game Mindset
3. Where to access further resources and support

Enemies.

This Workbook and the accompanying *Mindful Cricket* book address one fundamental problem:

....

Cricket is played above the shoulders, but there isn't a thorough yet simple framework to help players and coaches develop the mindset they need to be the best players they can be.

....

Even worse, our traditional approach to practising and playing the game leaves players ill-equipped to master the mental game of cricket.

Mindful Cricket addresses this problem by introducing the Game Mindset, which tackles this challenge head on by calling out the **four universal enemies** that not only cause us to under-perform as cricketers, but also to be less than we want to be in other aspects of our life:

- **Reactive Mind -** losing composure and letting unhelpful emotions take over
- **Distraction and Mind Drift -** being distracted from the present moment
- **Making It Complicated -** overthinking instead of keeping it simple
- **Slow to Change -** being slow and inflexible to learn and adapt to change.

Observe players who are battling these enemies. Batsmen seem rushed and off balance, bowlers are straining and spraying deliveries, and fielders look ragged and disorganised. They're out of control of their own space and the shape of their actions.

What have you learned about the ways these enemies affect your game?

Game Mindset.

Here is the mindset of nearly every cricketer who has consistently mastered his or her game in Tests, First-Class, club, school or courtyard cricket:

CLEAR MIND	Composed, Focused, Keeping It Simple and Adapting Fast
PLAY BRAVE	Bold Vision, Putting It On The Line, and Holding The Tension
PLAY CLEVER	Bringing cricket smarts to their game
PLAY BETTER	Applying a Growth Mindset, Game Ready and Optimistic.

That's it. And you'll see elements of this mindset in batsmen, bowlers, keepers and fielders in every game you watch from now on.

How have you seen Game Mindset displayed in other cricketers?

Where to From Here?

How can you use the simple practices and tools of Game Mindset to have the greatest possible impact on your own cricket enjoyment and performance, or use it to coach others? My suggestion is:

Access Resources	Read the *Mindful Cricket* book and regularly visit **www.mindfulcricket.com,** to find a growing range of resources and support to implement the principles, practices and activities of Game Mindset.
Get on the Pathway	Follow the five-step pathway below, and use practices like PDCA in net sessions to accelerate your learning and improvement.
Seek a Helping Hand	If you want a helping hand, then check in for some online coaching until you build your own momentum or create the breakthrough you want.

ACTIVITY: Five Steps Along the Pathway.

There are five steps which players and coaches find most effective, and the good news is you are ready now to put them into place, provided you are willing to devote time to achieve the benefits:

STEP 1: Know Your Blue Zone	Understand what's unique about your Game Mindset and how to trigger it to play Mindful Cricket.
STEP 2: Cultivate Composure	Build the foundation of calmness and composure, which underpin all other practices.
STEP 3: Focus in the Moment	Strengthen your ability to bring your mind into the present moment, where it's needed to make runs and take wickets.
STEP 4: Keep It Simple and Adapt Fast	Embrace this mindset to avoid the risks of making it complicated and being too slow to change.
STEP 5: Choose Your Priorities	Choose from the wide range of Mindful Cricket practices which are available to boost your Game Mindset.

STEP 1: Know Your Blue Zone.

The Blue Zone is the place to really get to know, because it reveals the blueprint for your unique Game Mindset, while reinforcing the value of a Clear Mind and Playing Brave, Playing Clever and Playing Better.

Practice Tip: Devote time to do the Activity to find your Blue Zone, because all the work you put in on Game Mindset is designed to get you into the Blue Zone.

STEP 2: Cultivate Composure.

Without composure the reactive mind is in charge, and that damages everything else. Begin with Cultivating Composure, and choose a Mindful Practice which helps to develop your Centred Breathing and calming skills.

Practice Tip: Find at least 10 minutes each day to practise creating the stillness and quiet observation of your breathing that will pay big dividends in those moments that matter.

STEP 3: Focus in the Moment.

Focus in the Moment is where the power of mindfulness is unlocked. When we truly stay in the moment, we play our best without getting in our own way or letting things outside our control detract from performance. Developing your ability to patiently bring your attention into the present has huge potential to boost your game.

Practice Tip: Develop and refine the 1-2-3 Reset for each aspect of your game, because every delivery needs a switch on or reset.

STEP 4: Keep It Simple and Adapt Fast.

Keep It Simple and Adapt Fast are fundamentally about the learning loop - the power of Plan, Do, Check and Adapt.

Your choice here depends on how serious you are about embracing Mindful Cricket as a way of life. If you want to deep dive, then read the *Mindful Cricket* book and visit the website to explore PDCA resources and support.

Practice Tip: Use PDCA at practice and combine it with a Go-To-Plan, because that's a great way to create a more match-like practice mindset and environment.

STEP 5: Choose Your Priorities.

With those foundations in place, the next move is yours to choose from the other nine principles:

Play Brave	Play Clever	Play Better
Create Your Bold Vision	Bat Smart	Apply A Growth Mindset
Put It On The Line	Bowl Smart	Be Game Ready
Hold The Tension	Keep And Field Smart	Bring Optimism

For each principle, there are examples of practices and activities in the book, and more are available online as we continue to build on ideas from the Mindful Cricket community.

Practice Tip: Choose one priority at a time to work on, and use the PDCA loop to Plan, Do, Check and Adapt until you are ready to move on to the next priority.

Resources and Support.

My hope in writing *Mindful Cricket* and the *Mindful Cricket Workbook* is for them to be just the starting points on a journey of helping cricketers and coaches to gain more enjoyment and success from the game.

At **www.mindfulcricket.com** there is a growing range of articles and tools, together with links to a range of courses we are building for coaches and players. These include our Coaching Mindful Cricket and Leading Mindful Cricket programs. The latter draws on resources and approaches we have developed at Think One Team Consulting (**www.thinkoneteam.com**) to help enterprises to set up their leadership teams and to foster an agile and adaptive way of operating.

A Final Word.

Cricket is a wonderful sport which prepares us all for the wider challenges of life. It can be maddeningly frustrating during a run of bad form, or wildly exhilarating when we win as a team or achieve a personal milestone.

Perhaps the greatest beauty of cricket is where and how it is played. I've been fortunate to travel and watch cricket played with all manner of equipment, in courtyards in Sri Lanka, in fields and on beaches in India, on manicured grounds in England and the Middle East, and in stadiums in Australia and New Zealand. On occasions I've glimpsed cricket in Malaysia, Singapore and Nepal, in Holland and Canada, and on a dusty road near the India-Pakistan border.

No matter where you play and with what equipment, cricket is always a game played above the shoulders. While cricket prepares us for life, I hope Mindful Cricket and the simplicity of the Game Mindset help prepare you to bring to the great game a Clear Mind and the attitude to Play Brave, Play Clever and Play Better, because that's the mindset you need to be the best cricketer you can be.

Good luck and good cricket.

References.

Dweck, CS 2008, *Mindset: The New Psychology of Success*, Ballantine Books, New York.

Ferriss, T 2007, *The 4-Hour Workweek, Expanded and Updated: Escape 9-5, Live Anywhere, and Join the New Rich (Expanded and Updated)*, read by Ray Porter, Blackstone Audio, Ashland.

Gallwey, WT 1979, *The Inner Game of Tennis*, Bantam Books, Toronto.

Gawande, A 2010, *The Checklist Manifesto: How to Get Things Right*, Metropolitan Books, New York.

Roosevelt, T 1910, *Citizenship in a Republic*, 23 April, Sorbonne, Paris.

Lightning Source UK Ltd.
Milton Keynes UK
UKHW031826050521
383192UK00008B/1669